Easy Excel 5
for Windows™

Trudi Reisner

Easy Excel 5 for Windows

Copyright © 1994 by Que® Corporation.

Library of Congress Catalog No.: 93-86746

ISBN: 1-56529-540-4

96 95   6 5 4

Interpretation of the printing code: the rightmost double-digit number is the year of the book's printing; the rightmost single-digit number, the number of the book's printing. For example, a printing code of 94-1 shows that the first printing of the book occurred in 1994.

Screen reproductions in this book were created with Collage Plus from Inner Media, Inc., Hollis, NH.

Publisher: David P. Ewing

Director of Publishing: Michael Miller

Managing Editor: Corinne Walls

Marketing Manager: Ray Robinson

Credits

Publishing Manager
Don Roche, Jr.

Acquisitions Editor
Nancy Stevenson

Product Directors
Joyce J. Nielsen
Robin Drake

Production Editor
Michael Cunningham

Editors
Linda Seifert
Pamela Wampler

Technical Editor
Richard F. Brown

Novice Reviewer
Paul Marchesseault

Book Designer
Amy Peppler-Adams

Cover Designer
Jay Corpus

Production Team
Angela Bannan
Claudia Bell
Danielle Bird
Paula Carroll
Anne Dickerson
Teresa Forrester
Joelynn Gifford
Bob LaRoche
Beth Lewis
Tim Montgomery
Nanci Sears Perry
Dennis Sheehan
Amy Steed
Sue VandeWalle
Mary Beth Wakefield
Michelle Worthington
Lillian Yates

Indexers
Jeannie Clark
Johnna VanHoose

Composed in *Stone* and *MCPdigital* by Que Corporation

About the Author

Trudi Reisner is a computer consultant specializing in training users of IBM PCs, PC compatibles, and Apple Macintoshes in the use of applications software. She is the owner of Computer Training Solutions, a Boston, Massachusetts, company that offers training, technical writing, curriculum development, and consulting services in software programs.

Trudi has written more than 15 books on Excel and other software, including *Ami Pro 3 Quick Reference, Harvard Graphics 3 Quick Reference, Quattro Pro 4 Quick Reference, Word for Windows 2 Quick Reference, Easy 1-2-3 for Windows, Easy Ami Pro 3.1, Easy Word 6 for Windows, Easy WordPerfect 6 for Windows, Easy Microsoft Office, Excel for Windows VisiRef, and Windows 3.11 VisiRef*. She is also a contributing author to *Using Ami Pro 3 for Windows*, Special Edition.

Dedication

To Robert L. Jones III, with special thanks for his encouragement and support.

Acknowledgments

I owe thanks to many others who helped complete this book. Foremost is Joyce Nielsen, a Product Development Specialist at Que, who developed the manuscript and gave suggestions and support throughout the life of this project; and Michael Cunningham, Senior Editor/Team Leader at Que, who managed the copyediting process for this project. Special thanks to Don Roche, Publishing Manager, for his guidance in the structure and design of this book. Special recognition must go to Nancy Stevenson, Acquisitions Editor at Que, who suggested the project.

Also, many thanks to the technical editors, whose timely proofing helped maintain the accuracy of the text from cover to cover. Special thanks to the production staff who turned the final draft on disk into this printed copy in record time—a monumental task.

Finally, thanks to Microsoft Corporation, who developed and produced a fine spreadsheet program. Also, thanks to each person on the technical support team who answered technical questions about Excel 5 for Windows.

Trademark Acknowledgments

All terms mentioned in this book that are known to be trademarks or service marks have been appropriately capitalized. Que Corporation cannot attest to the accuracy of this information. Use of a term in this book should not be regarded as affecting the validity of any trademark or service mark.

Contents at a Glance

Contents

Part III: Working with Formulas   86

Part IV: Managing Files   116

Part V: Formatting the Worksheet   134

Part VI: Printing the Worksheet   164

Part VII: Working with Charts — 182

Part VIII: Sample Documents — 220

Part IX: Reference 232

Index 238

Introduction

Introduction

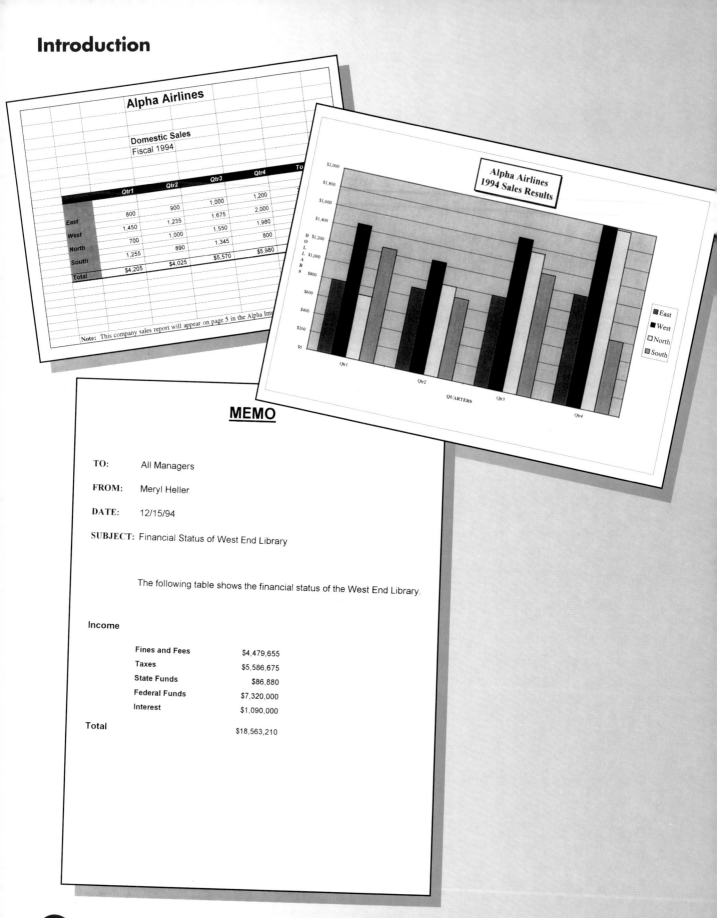

Alpha Airlines

Domestic Sales
Fiscal 1994

	Qtr1	Qtr2	Qtr3	Qtr4	To...
			1,000	1,200	
	800	900	1,675	2,000	
East	1,450	1,235	1,550	1,980	
West	700	1,000	1,345	800	
North	1,255	890		$5,980	
South			$5,570		
Total	$4,205	$4,025			

Note: This company sales report will appear on page 5 in the Alpha Int...

**Alpha Airlines
1994 Sales Results**

(bar chart with legend: East, West, North, South; axis DOLLARS $0–$2,000; QUARTERS Qtr1, Qtr2, Qtr3, Qtr4)

MEMO

TO: All Managers

FROM: Meryl Heller

DATE: 12/15/94

SUBJECT: Financial Status of West End Library

The following table shows the financial status of the West End Library.

Income

Fines and Fees	$4,479,655
Taxes	$5,586,675
State Funds	$86,880
Federal Funds	$7,320,000
Interest	$1,090,000

Total $18,563,210

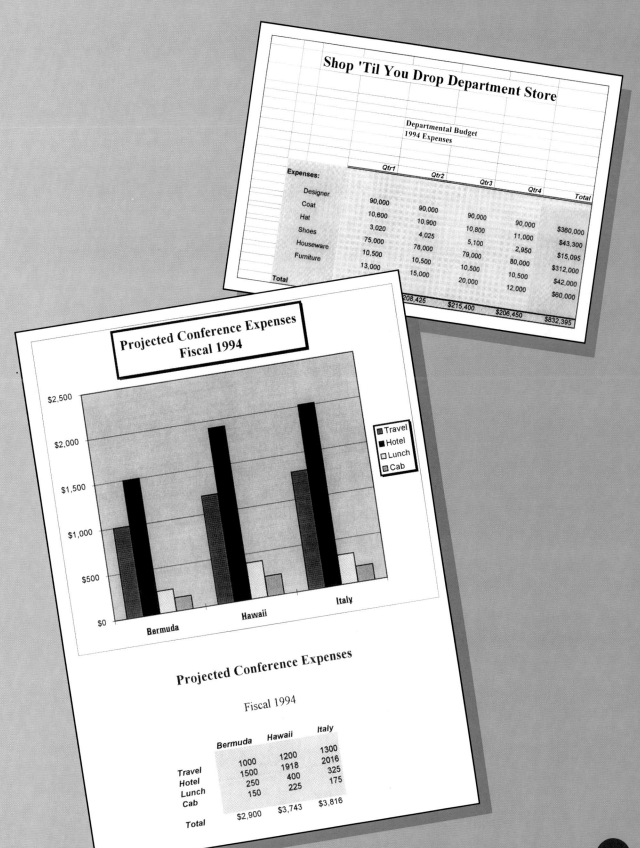

What You Can Do with Excel

Microsoft Excel is one of the world's most popular spreadsheet software programs. You could create worksheets on ledger paper and use a calculator, or draw charts on graph paper, but Excel makes managing numeric information easier. You can use the program to create worksheets, databases, charts, and macros.

Specifically, you can use Excel to perform these functions:

- *Lay out a worksheet.* When you sit down to develop a worksheet with a pencil and ledger paper, you don't always have all the information to complete the design and layout of the worksheet. Ideas may occur to you after you sketch the layout of your worksheet. After you're finished jotting down the column headings and the row headings, you might think of another column or row you didn't include. With Excel, you can insert columns and rows easily and move data from one location to another.

- *Calculate numbers.* If you have a checkbook register, you subtract the amount of each check written and add the deposits to the running balance. When you receive your bank statement and balance your checkbook, you might find that you made math errors in your checkbook. In this case, you must erase the old answers, recalculate the numbers, and jot down the new answers. In Excel, you enter a formula once. Then, when you change the numbers in the worksheet, Excel recalculates the formulas instantly and gives you the new answers.

- *Make editing changes.* To correct a mistake on ledger paper, you have to use an eraser, or reconstruct the entire worksheet. With Excel, you can overwrite data in any cell in your worksheet. You can also delete data quickly—in one cell or a range of cells.

- *Undo mistakes.* When you accidentally delete data that you want to keep, you don't have to retype it. Instead, you can just restore the data with the Undo feature. You can also use the Undo command to reverse the last command or action.

- *Check spelling.* Before you print, you can run a spell check to search for misspellings. If you are a poor typist, this feature enables you to concentrate on calculating your numbers and leaves catching spelling errors for Excel.

- *View data.* When working with a large worksheet, such as a financial statement, you might have to use a ruler to compare figures on a far portion of the worksheet on ledger paper. In Excel, you can split the worksheet into two panes to view distant figures side by side. That way, you can easily see the effects of playing "what if?" scenarios to project changes and then make the necessary adjustments.

■ *Make formatting changes.* Excel easily enables you to align data in cells, center column headings across columns, adjust column width, display numbers with dollar signs, commas, and decimal points, and other formatting options. You can experiment with the settings until the worksheet appears the way that you want it, then you can print it.

■ *Change how data is printed.* You can boldface, italicize, and underline data. Excel also lets you shade cells and add borders. You can also use a different typeface, depending on your printer.

■ *Preview your print job.* You can preview your worksheet to see how it will look when you print it. If you want to make changes before you print, you also can do this in print preview.

■ *Sort data.* You can sort data on the worksheet alphabetically and numerically in ascending or descending order. For example, you can sort a customer invoice report in chronological order by dates.

■ *Chart numeric data.* You can track the sales trends of several products with an embedded column chart. Make as many "what if?" projections as you want in the worksheet by increasing and decreasing the numbers. As you change the numbers in the worksheet, Excel instantly updates the embedded chart. Excel's embedded charts let you view simultaneously the sales trends in a picture representation on-screen and the numbers in the worksheet, making your sales forecasting more efficient.

■ *Organize lists.* You can create a database to organize your data in a list, such as inventory, employee lists, customer lists, sales records, and so on. In Excel, you can add, delete, sort, search, and display records in the list as often as required to maintain the list.

Task Sections

The Task sections include numbered steps that tell you how to accomplish certain tasks, such as saving a workbook or filling a range. The numbered steps walk you through a specific example so that you can learn the task by actually doing it.

Big Screen

At the beginning of each task is a large screen shot that shows how the computer screen will look after you complete the procedure that follows in that task. Sometimes the screen shot shows a feature discussed in that task, however, such as a shortcut menu.

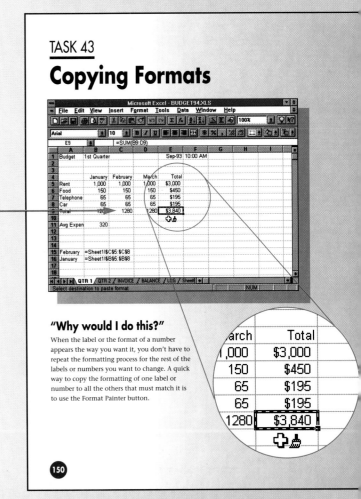

TASK 43

Copying Formats

"Why would I do this?"

When the label or the format of a number appears the way you want it, you don't have to repeat the formatting process for the rest of the labels or numbers you want to change. A quick way to copy the formatting of one label or number to all the others that must match it is to use the Format Painter button.

Step-by-Step Screens

Each task includes a screen shot for each step of a procedure. The screen shot shows how the computer screen looks at each step in the process.

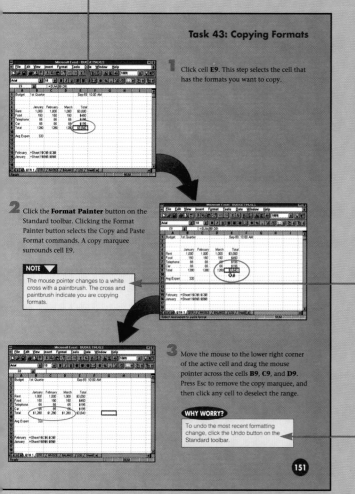

Task 43: Copying Formats

1 Click cell **E9**. This step selects the cell that has the formats you want to copy.

2 Click the **Format Painter** button on the Standard toolbar. Clicking the Format Painter button selects the Copy and Paste Format commands. A copy marquee surrounds cell E9.

NOTE ▼
The mouse pointer changes to a white cross with a paintbrush. The cross and paintbrush indicate you are copying formats.

3 Move the mouse to the lower right corner of the active cell and drag the mouse pointer across the cells **B9**, **C9**, and **D9**. Press Esc to remove the copy marquee, and then click any cell to deselect the range.

WHY WORRY?
To undo the most recent formatting change, click the Undo button on the Standard toolbar.

151

Other Notes

Many tasks include other short notes that tell you a little more about certain procedures. These notes define terms, explain other options, refer you to other sections when applicable, and so on.

Why Worry? Notes

You may find that you performed a task, such as sorting data, that you didn't want to do after all. The Why Worry? notes tell you how to undo certain procedures or get out of a situation, such as displaying a Help screen.

PART I
The Basics

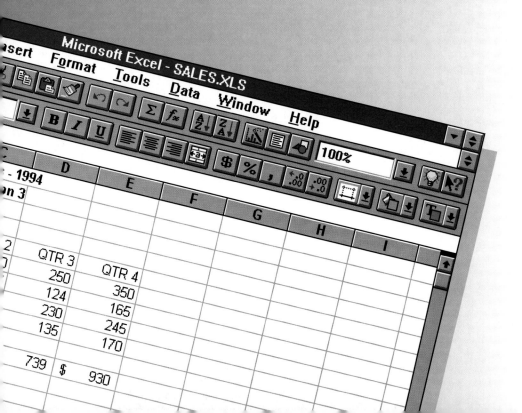

Part I of this book introduces you to Excel basics. You need to know some fundamental things about Excel before you start creating your own worksheets.

In this part, you will learn how to start and exit Excel. You should ensure that Excel is installed on your hard disk so that it appears in your Windows Program Manager as a program icon. For installation instructions, refer to your Microsoft Excel Version 5 for Windows documentation. You can start and exit Excel as you would any Windows application.

When you start the program, Excel displays a blank *workbook*. The workbook is a file in which you store your data, similar to a three-ring binder. Within a workbook, you have *sheets*, such as worksheets, chart sheets, and macro sheets. A new workbook contains 16 sheets, named Sheet 1 through Sheet 16. You can have up to 255 sheets per workbook, depending on your computer's available memory. Multiple sheets help you organize, manage, and consolidate your data. For example, you might want to create a sales forecast for the first quarter of the year. Sheet1, Sheet2, and Sheet3 contain worksheet data for January, February, and March; Sheet4 contains a summary for the three months of sales data, and Sheet5 contains a chart showing sales over the three-month period.

A *worksheet* is a grid of columns and rows. The intersection of any column and row is called a *cell*. Each cell in a worksheet has a unique cell address. A cell address is the designation formed by combining the row and column names. For example, A8 is the address of the cell at the intersection of column A and row 8.

The *cell pointer* is a cross-shaped pointer that appears over cells in the worksheet. You use the cell pointer to select any cell in the worksheet. The selected cell is called the *active cell*. You always have at least one cell selected at all times.

A *range* is a specified group of cells. A range can be a single cell, a column, a row, or any combination of cells, columns, and rows. *Range coordinates* identify a range. The first element in the range coordinates is the location of the uppermost left cell in the range; the second element is the location of the lowermost right cell. A colon (:) separates these two elements. For example, the range A1:C3 includes the cells A1, A2, A3, B1, B2, B3, C1, C2, and C3.

The worksheet is much larger than one screen can possibly display at one time. To place data in the many cells that make up the worksheet, you must be able to move to the desired locations. There are many ways to move around the worksheet. You can use the arrow keys to move one cell at a time. You can also use key combinations to quickly move around the worksheet. When you move the cell pointer to a cell, that cell becomes the active cell. The active cell has a dark border around the cell.

You can navigate around the worksheet with the following arrow keys and key combinations:

To move	Press
Right one cell	→
Left one cell	←
Up one cell	↑
Down one cell	↓
To the beginning of a row	**Home**
To the end of a row	**End**+→
To the first cell (A1)	**Ctrl**+**Home**
To the last cell (containing data)	**Ctrl**+**End**

In this part, you will learn how to use the shortcut menus. When you point to a single cell or a selected range of cells and then click the right mouse button, Excel displays a shortcut menu. This menu appears next to the cell or selected range of cells. Shortcut menus contain fewer commands than a menu in the menu bar. The commands on the shortcut menus vary, depending on the cells or object you select in the worksheet. You might find it quicker and easier to use a shortcut menu rather than select commands from the menu bar and the pull-down menus.

You also learn how to use the toolbar. Excel ships with many different toolbars that include the tools you use for formatting a worksheet, creating a chart, drawing graphics on the worksheet, creating macros, and many other Excel operations. Sometimes you might want to have a clean screen or you may want to make more rows in a worksheet visible. You can hide the toolbars to make more room on-screen. This part also discusses some of the ways you can get help in Excel. You can get instant on-line Help, look at the Quick Preview, Examples and Demos, sample files, and view the TipWizard.

Starting and Exiting Excel

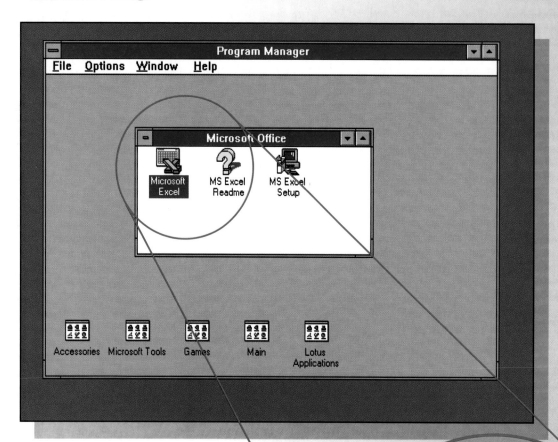

"Why would I do this?"

Starting Excel is simple to do—once you've done it, it's as easy as starting the engine in your car! When you no longer want to work in Excel, you can exit Excel and return to the Windows Program Manager.

This task assumes you have turned on your computer and monitor and started Microsoft Windows. The Program Manager appears in a window on-screen.

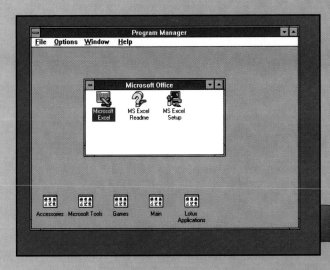

1 Double-click the group icon for **Microsoft Office**. The group icon is the icon for the program group where you stored Excel when you installed the program. To double-click the group icon, move the mouse pointer to the group icon and click the left mouse button twice in rapid succession.

NOTE ▼

If the program group is maximized, you only need to click the existing program group to make it active, not double-click the group icon.

2 Double-click the program icon for **Microsoft Excel**. This step starts the Excel program. A blank workbook appears in a window on-screen.

WHY WORRY?

When you're using the mouse to execute a command, make sure you double-click the left mouse button. If nothing happens, check the location of the mouse pointer and try double-clicking again.

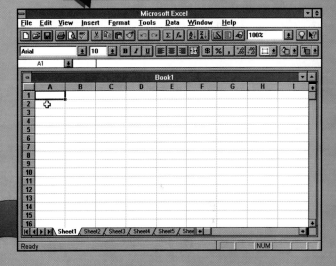

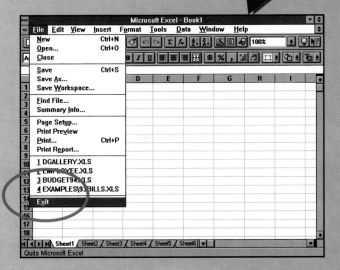

3 Click **File** in the menu bar. Then, click **Exit**. This step selects the **File Exit** command. You return to the Windows Program Manager.

NOTE ▼

To quickly exit Excel, double-click the Control-menu box. This box is the small bar to the left of the Excel window's title bar, in the upper left corner of the screen.

TASK 2

Using Shortcut Menus

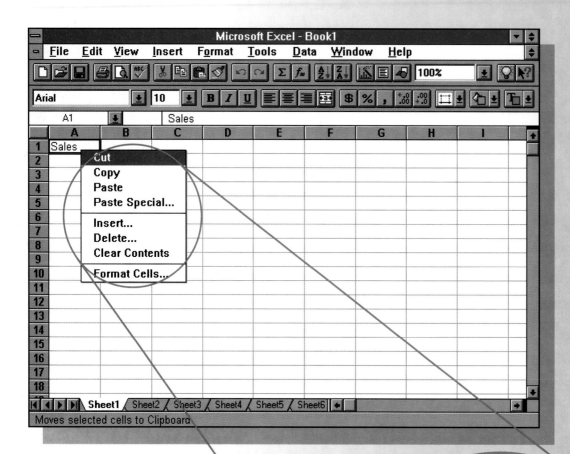

"Why would I do this?"

Excel's shortcut menus include just those commands you need to use for the currently selected cell(s) or an object such as a chart. You might want to use a shortcut menu to quickly edit or format cells.

Let's take a look at a shortcut menu that contains editing and formatting commands.

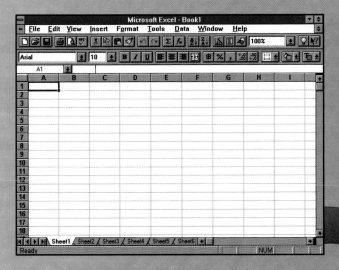

1 Start Excel. If you need help with this step, see Task 1: Starting and Exiting Excel.

2 Type **Sales** and press **Enter**. This step enters Sales into cell A1 and makes cell A2 the active cell.

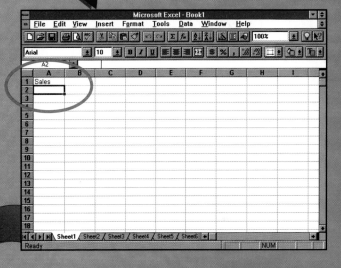

3 Click cell **A1**. This step selects cell A1, making A1 the active cell—the cell in which you want to open the shortcut menu.

Task 2: Using Shortcut Menus

4 Point to inside cell **A1** and click the right mouse button. This step opens the shortcut menu. Excel displays a list of editing and formatting commands.

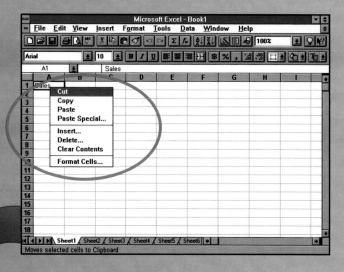

5 Click **Clear Contents**. This step selects the Clear Contents command, which erases the contents of cell A1. The shortcut menu disappears.

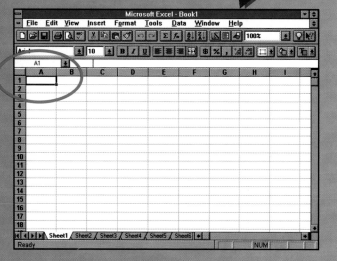

WHY WORRY?

Sometimes you may display a shortcut menu that doesn't have the command you want to use. To leave a shortcut menu without making a selection, press the Esc key.

TASK 3
Using the Toolbar

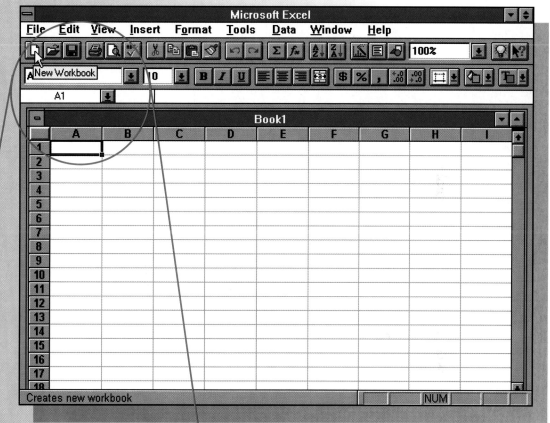

"Why would I do this?"

The Standard toolbar contains buttons for the most common Excel commands. The Formatting toolbar contains lists and buttons for the most common formatting commands. You must have a mouse to use the toolbars. To perform tasks quickly, you select a toolbar button rather than a menu command. When you leave the mouse pointer on a toolbar button, Excel displays the button name near the button.

Task 3: Using the Toolbar

1 Point to the New Workbook button, the first button from the left on the Standard toolbar, and leave the mouse pointer on the button. This step displays the button's name, New Workbook, in a yellow box near the button. This is the ToolTip feature.

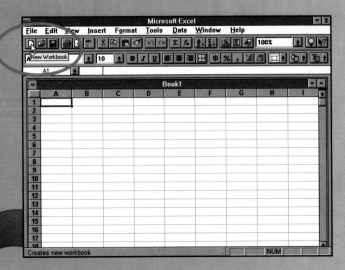

2 Click the **New Workbook** button. Excel opens a new workbook and displays Book2 on top of Book1.

WHY WORRY?

Be sure to move the mouse pointer directly over the toolbar button. If the ToolTip does not appear, try moving the mouse pointer again and pause a few seconds.

3 Click **File** in the menu bar. Then click **Close**. Excel closes the Book2 workbook. Book1 is the active workbook.

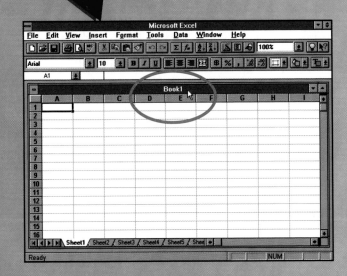

Getting Help

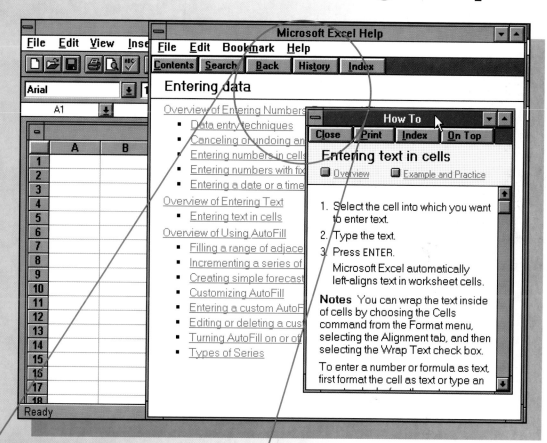

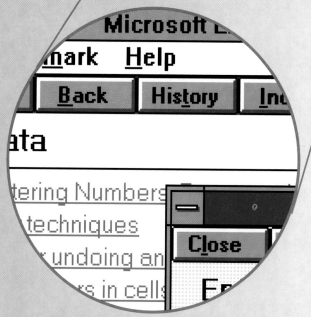

"Why would I do this?"

Excel offers many ways to get help, and the Help feature has its own menu system. Excel's new TipWizard is an intuitive feature that lets you know when there is a quicker or better way to perform an action that you just performed.

First, let's get some help on how to enter text in cells. Next, we enter data and then undo the entry. Finally, we will use the TipWizard to get a tip for undoing the entry.

Task 4: Getting Help

1 Click **Help** in the menu bar. Then click **Contents**. Excel opens the Help window. The name of the Help window appears in the title bar.

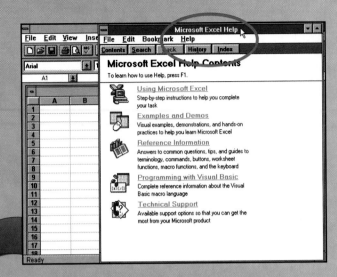

2 Point to **Using Microsoft Excel** and click the left mouse button. This step displays a list of topics.

> **NOTE** ▼
>
> When the mouse pointer is on a topic for which you can get help, the pointer changes to a hand with a pointing finger.

3 Point to the topic **Essential Skills** and click the left mouse button. This step selects the Help topic and displays a list of subtopics.

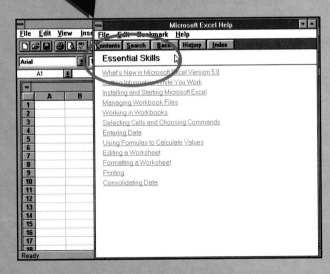

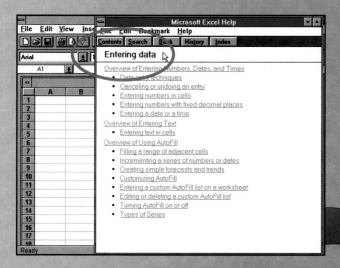

4 Point to the topic **Entering Data** and click the left mouse button. This step selects the Help topic and displays a list of more subtopics.

5 Point to the topic **Entering text in cells** and click the left mouse button. This step selects the Help topic and opens the How To dialog box. This dialog box contains the steps you follow to enter text in cells.

NOTE ▼

You can also click the Help button in a dialog box to get help on the command for which you are setting options.

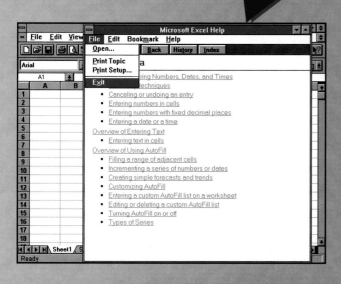

6 Click the **Close** button in the How To dialog box. Next, click **File** in the Help window's menu bar. Then click **Exit**. Excel closes the How To dialog box, selects the Exit command, and then closes the Help window.

7 Click cell **A1** and type **sunny** and press **Enter**. This step enters *sunny* into cell A1.

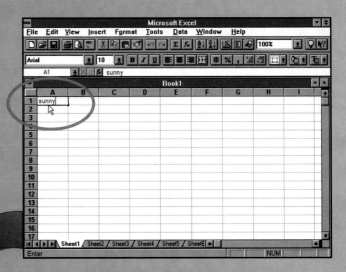

8 Click **Edit** in the menu bar, and then click **Undo Entry**. This step undoes the entry. Notice that the TipWizard button, which is the light bulb near the right end of the Standard toolbar, appears in bright yellow.

> **NOTE** ▼
>
> If the TipWizard button does not light up after you perform an action, then Excel does not have a tip for the action you just performed.

9 Click the **TipWizard** button. Excel displays the TipWizard toolbar. A tip on how to Undo quickly and more efficiently appears in the TipWizard. Because it is mentioned in the tip, the Undo button appears to the right of the TipWizard toolbar. The Undo button has a left-pointing curved arrow.

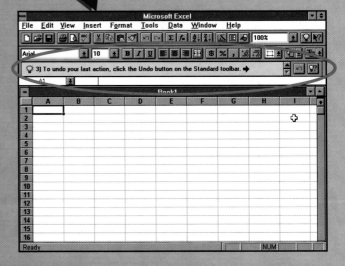

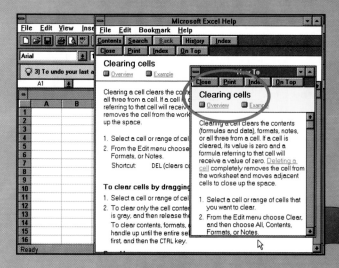

10 Click the **Tip Help** button (the light bulb with a question mark near the right end of the TipWizard toolbar). This step displays Help information on a related feature, Clearing Cells. Click the **Close** button in the How To dialog box and then choose the **File Exit** command to close the Help window.

11 Click the **TipWizard** button. Excel closes the TipWizard toolbar.

NOTE ▼

When the TipWizard toolbar is displayed, you can click the up- and down-arrow buttons on the TipWizard toolbar to scroll through the list of tips that have appeared during the current session.

WHY WORRY?

To shut the Excel help window quickly, double-click the Control-menu box. This box is the small bar to the left of the window's title bar.

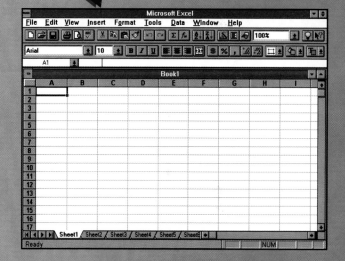

TASK 5

Moving Around the Worksheet

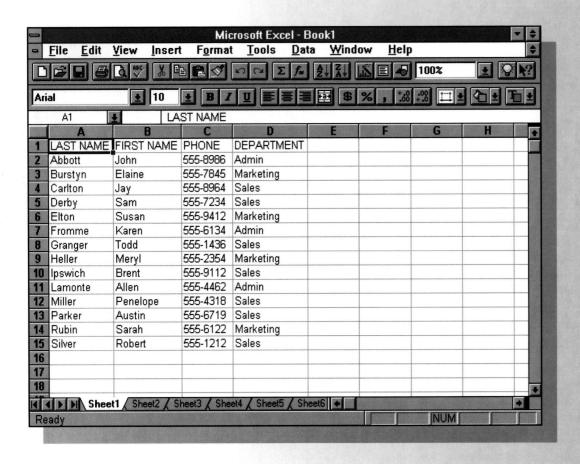

"Why would I do this?"

Because you typically use many cells in a worksheet, you need shortcuts for moving around the worksheet. Using a mouse is often the easiest way to move around the worksheet—simply use the vertical or horizontal scroll bar to see other portions of the worksheet.

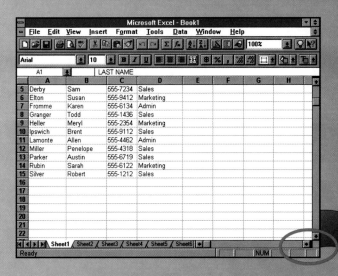

1 Click four times on the down scroll arrow at the bottom of the vertical scroll bar. Clicking the down scroll arrow moves the worksheet down one row at a time. Notice that row 5 appears at the top of the worksheet.

NOTE ▼

You can point to the up, down, left, or right scroll bar arrow and hold down the mouse button to scroll the worksheet continuously in a particular direction.

2 Click three times on the up scroll arrow at the top of the vertical scroll bar. Clicking the up scroll arrow scrolls the worksheet up one row at a time Notice that row 2 appears at the top of the worksheet.

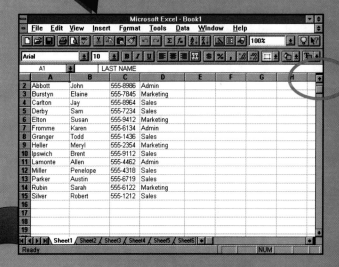

3 Click half-way down in the vertical scroll bar itself. Clicking in the scroll bar moves the worksheet up or down one screen at a time. Notice that row 20 appears at the top of the worksheet and the scroll box is at the bottom of the vertical scroll bar.

Task 5: Moving Around the Worksheet

4 Drag the scroll box up to the top of the vertical scroll bar. Dragging the scroll box moves the worksheet quickly to a new location in the direction of the scroll box. In this case, Excel moves the worksheet up to the top of the screen and displays the beginning of the worksheet.

NOTE ▼

Keep in mind that whatever scroll bar action you perform on a vertical scroll bar can also be performed on the horizontal scroll bar.

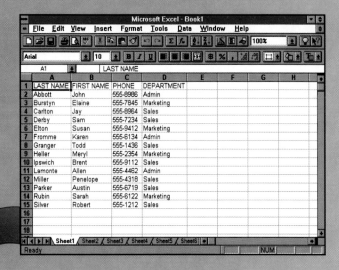

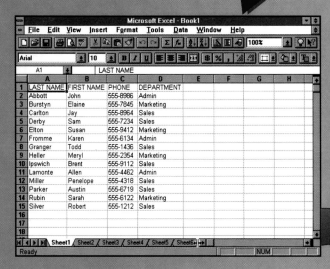

5 Move the mouse pointer to the tab split box, the vertical bar located to the left of the horizontal scroll arrow. The mouse pointer changes to a vertical bar with a left and a right arrow.

WHY WORRY?

If you run out of room to move the mouse on your desktop or mouse pad, just lift the mouse and then put it down. The mouse pointer will not move when the mouse is in the air. Then try moving the mouse again.

6 Drag the tab split box to the left until the box is aligned with the right edge of the Sheet3 tab. Dragging the tab split box to the left displays more of the horizontal scroll bar and fewer sheet tabs. In this case, you see the Sheet1, Sheet2, and Sheet3 tabs and more of the horizontal scroll bar. (You can double-click the tab split box to restore the sheet tabs and horizontal scroll to their original display.)

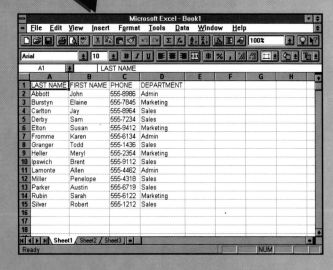

Moving Between Worksheets

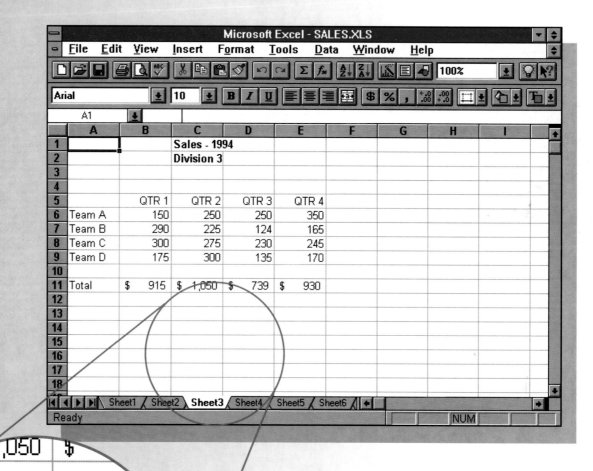

"Why would I do this?"

Suppose all the sheets relating to inventory are stored in one workbook. Before you make changes to these sheets, you will need to move from sheet to sheet to find the sheet you want to view or change. You can use the *tab scrolling buttons* to move between worksheets. The tab scrolling buttons are the four buttons that appear to the left of the sheet tabs. After you make a sheet visible, you can select it so that you can work on the sheet.

Task 6: Moving Between Worksheets

1 Notice there are four tab scrolling buttons to the left of the sheet tabs. Click twice on the **Next Tab** scrolling button (the third button—with a right arrow on it).

Clicking the Next Tab scrolling button scrolls the sheets to display one more sheet tab to the right. In this case, clicking twice hides the Sheet1 and Sheet2 tabs and displays the Sheet3, Sheet4, Sheet5, Sheet6, Sheet7, and Sheet8 tabs.

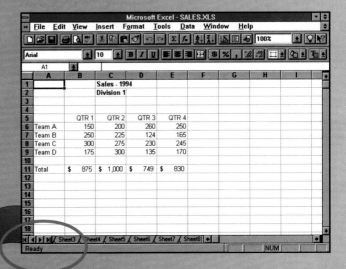

2 Click twice on the **Previous Tab** scrolling button (the second button—with a left arrow on it). Clicking the Previous Tab scrolling button scrolls the sheets to display one more sheet tab to the left. In this case, clicking twice redisplays the Sheet1 and Sheet2 tabs.

> **NOTE** ▼
>
> You can also hold down the Shift key and click the Previous Tab scrolling button (the second button) to scroll the sheets and display several sheet tabs to the left at one time.

3 Hold down the **Shift** key and click the **Next Tab** scrolling button (the third button). Holding down the Shift key and clicking the Next Tab scrolling button scrolls the sheets to display several sheet tabs to the right at one time. As you can see, Excel displays the Sheet6, Sheet7, Sheet8, Sheet9, Sheet10, and Sheet11 tabs.

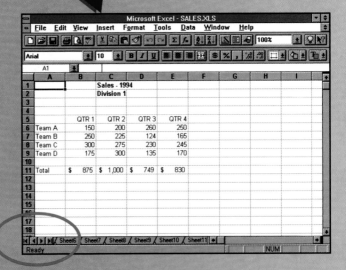

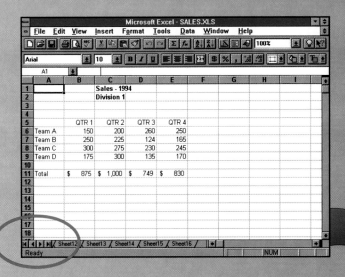

4 Click the **Last Tab** scrolling button (the last button—with a right arrow and a vertical bar). Clicking the Last Tab scrolling button displays the last sheet tab in the workbook. Notice the last sheet tab is Sheet16.

5 Click the **First Tab** scrolling button (the first button—with a left arrow and a vertical bar). Clicking the First Tab scrolling button displays the first sheet tab in the workbook. Excel redisplays the Sheet1, Sheet2, Sheet3, Sheet4, Sheet5, and Sheet6 tabs.

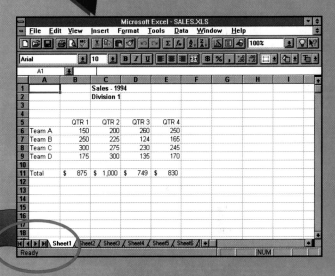

6 Click the **Sheet3** tab. Excel moves this sheet to the top and makes it the active sheet. You can click any of the tabs to make a sheet active.

WHY WORRY?

If you accidentally move to the wrong sheet, click a different tab scrolling button that moves to the sheet you want to view in the workbook. If you selected the wrong sheet, just click the correct sheet tab.

Moving to a Specific Cell

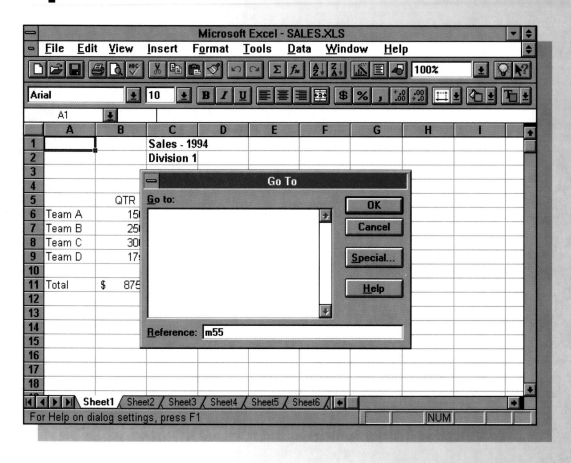

"Why would I do this?"

The Go To command is useful for jumping to cells that are out of view. You can also use the Go To command to select a range of cells. A range of cells is referenced by its first and last cells, separated by a colon. For example, B5:E8 references the uppermost left cell B5 and the lowermost right cell E8. This range starts with cell B5, continues across columns C, D, and E, continues down rows 6, 7, and 8, and ends at cell E8.

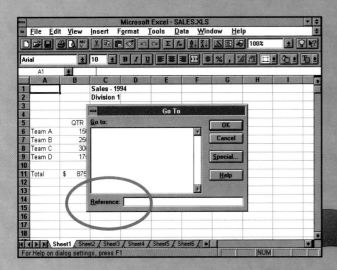

1 Press **F5**. F5 is the Go To key. Pressing F5 selects the Go To command. Excel opens the Go To dialog box. The insertion point is in the Reference text box.

2 Type **M55**. M55 is the cell to which you want to go. Remember that cells are referenced by their column letter and row number.

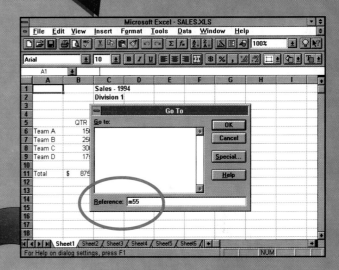

3 Press **Enter**. When you press Enter, M55 becomes the active cell.

Task 7: Moving to a Specific Cell

4 Click cell **E40**. E40 becomes the active cell. This is the first cell in the range you want to select.

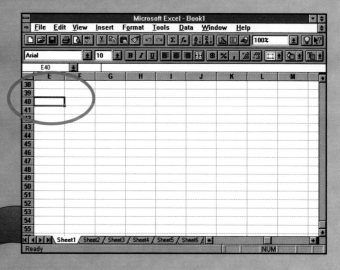

5 Hold down the mouse button and drag the mouse down the column to select cells **E40**, **E41**, **E42**, **E43**, **E44**, and **E45**. Then release the mouse button. This step selects the range E40:E45. A range is indicated by the address of the upper left cell, a colon (:), and the address of the lower right cell.

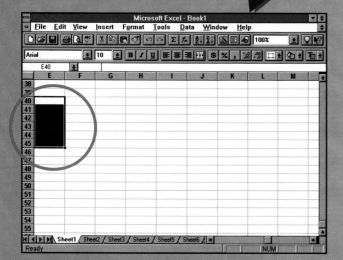

WHY WORRY?

If you mistakenly moved to the wrong cell reference, repeat the Go To command to move to the correct cell. If you selected the wrong range, click any cell to deselect the range. Then try again.

TASK 8

Selecting Cells

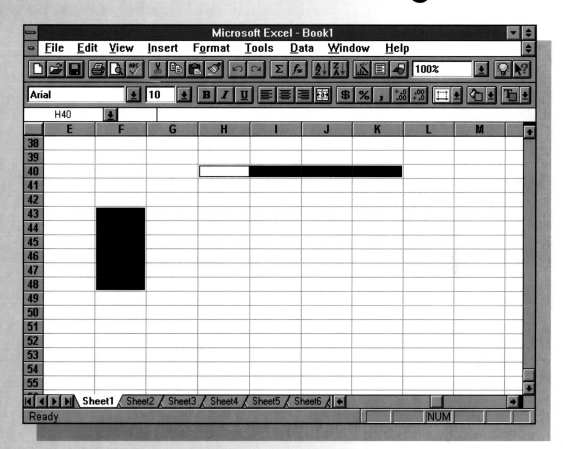

"Why would I do this?"

Knowing how to select a cell is essential because most of the commands and options in Excel operate on the selected cell. You can also select a *range*—a group of adjacent cells. You can even select several ranges at one time with the mouse. For example, there are times when you may want to perform a command on a group of cells that are not adjacent. Maybe you want to change the alignment of text in the top row of the worksheet and a column along the side. To make the change to both ranges, you need to select both ranges at the same time.

Task 8: Selecting Cells

1 Click cell **G40**. G40 becomes the active cell.

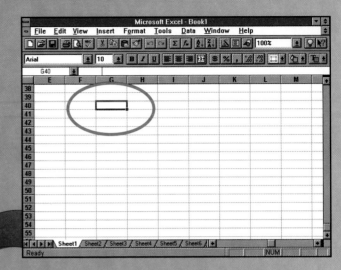

2 Hold down the mouse button and drag the mouse to select cells **F43**, **F44**, **F45**, **F46**, **F47**, and **F48**. This step deselects cell G40 and selects the range F43:F48.

3 Hold down the **Ctrl** key and select **H40**, then drag the mouse to select cells **I40**, **J40**, and **K40**. Release the mouse button and then release the **Ctrl** key. Notice the first range F43:F48 remains selected and the second range H40:K40 is also selected.

WHY WORRY?

If you selected the wrong cell, click the correct cell. If you selected the wrong range, click any cell to deselect the range.

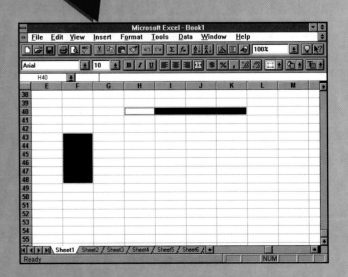

PART II

Entering and Editing Data

There are four types of data you can enter into an Excel worksheet: text, numbers, calculations, and dates. Text entries are sometimes called *labels*. Excel aligns labels with the left side of a cell. Labels can contain letters, symbols, numbers, or any combination of these characters. When a text entry contains numbers, Excel cannot use it for numeric calculations.

An example of a label is a title to describe the type of worksheet you want to create. A title such as 1994 ANNUAL BUDGET gives meaning to the columns and rows of numbers that make up a budget worksheet. Column headings describe what the numbers represent in a column. You can enter column headings to specify time periods such as years, months, days, dates, and so on. Row headings describe what the numbers represent in a row. You can enter row headings to identify income and expense items in a budget, subject titles, and other categories.

Numeric entries are sometimes called *values*. Excel aligns values with the right side of a cell. Values contain numbers and other symbols. Numeric entries must begin with a numeral or one of the following symbols: +, −, (, ., or $. The period is used as a decimal point for decimal values. You might find it quicker to enter numeric data by typing the numbers and using the Enter key on your numeric keypad. Numbers are useful for making calculations. For instance, Excel can recognize the number in a cell and add it to the number in a different cell.

In Excel, calculations are called *formulas*. Excel displays the result of a formula in a cell as a numeric value and aligns it with the right side of a cell.

Dates are recognized by Excel as values and appear aligned with the right side of a cell. Dates in a worksheet can help you keep track of the last time you modified your worksheet. You can also enter dates in a report to show when items are posted or when transactions are done. Excel recognizes an entry as a valid date only if you enter the date in one of the date formats accepted by Excel. The following table shows the Excel date formats you would enter in a cell and sample results:

Format	Example
MM/DD/YY	9/12/94
DD-MMM-YY	12-Sep-94
DD-MMM	12-Sep (assumes the current year)
MMM-YY	Sep-94 (assumes the first day of the month)

Times are treated the same way as dates by Excel. Time entries are values and appear aligned with the right side of a cell. Entering a time in a worksheet is especially useful for keeping track of the last time you worked on the worksheet. Another example is when you want to create a time table or time study. Excel recognizes an entry as a valid time only if you enter the time in one of the time formats accepted by Excel. The following table shows the Excel time formats you would enter in a cell and sample results:

Format	Example
HH:MM	13:45 (24-hour clock)
HH:MM AM/PM	2:45 AM (12-hour clock)
HH:MM:SS	13:45:06 (24-hour clock)
HH:MM:SS AM/PM	2:45:06 PM (12-hour clock)

There are three methods for entering data in an Excel worksheet: 1) type the data and press Enter, 2) type the data and press an arrow key, and 3) type the data and click the check mark in the formula bar. The formula bar is located beneath the Formatting toolbar. When you enter data in a cell, Excel displays an X and a check mark in the formula bar. If you click the X, Excel rejects the entry; if you click the check mark, Excel accepts the entry.

After you enter data, you can undo mistakes, overwrite a cell, edit the information in a cell, erase data, copy information, and move data to other locations in the worksheet. You also can insert and delete cells, rows, and columns.

Entering Text and Numbers

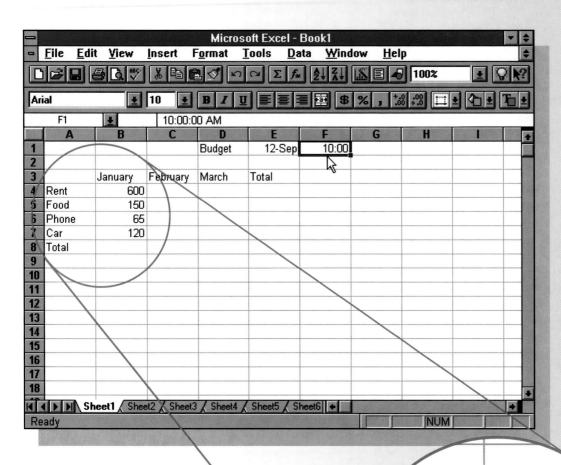

"Why would I do this?"

To give meaning to the columns and rows of numbers that make up a worksheet, you can give them names to describe what the numbers represent. Excel calls these names *labels*.

After you label the worksheet, you enter numbers into the appropriate cells. Excel also lets you enter dates and times in a worksheet.

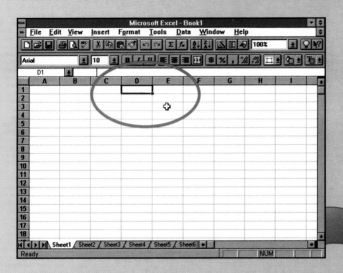

1 Point to cell **D1** and click. This step makes D1 the active cell. The active cell on a worksheet appears as a white cell with a bold border. When the mouse pointer is within the worksheet, the pointer appears as a cross.

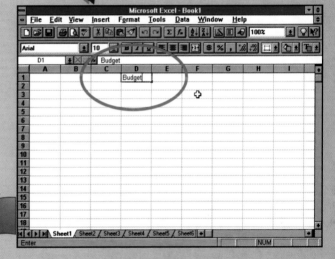

2 Type **Budget**. This is the title of your worksheet. Notice that the entry appears in the formula bar and in cell D1. The mode indicator in the lower left corner of the screen displays Enter.

NOTE ▼

An X and a check mark appear before the entry in the formula bar. Clicking the X cancels the change; clicking the check mark confirms the new entry.

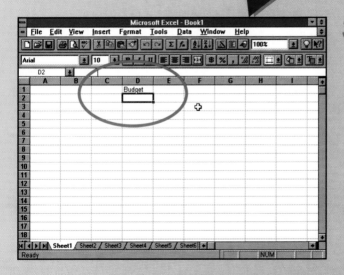

3 Press **Enter**. Pressing Enter accepts the entry in the formula bar, enters it into the cell, and makes D2 the active cell. Notice that Budget is left-aligned.

NOTE ▼

Excel always moves down one cell when you type data and press Enter.

Task 9: Entering Text and Numbers

4 Select cell **B3**. This cell is where you will enter a label for the first column heading.

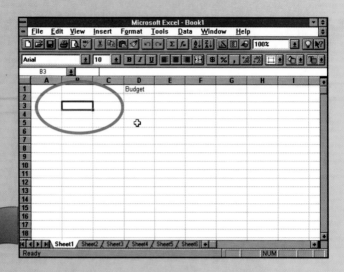

5 Type **January** and press the right-arrow key (→). Pressing the right-arrow key accepts the entry, enters the label into the cell, and makes C3 the active cell.

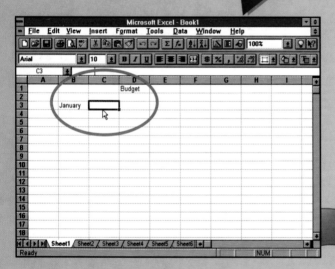

WHY WORRY?

If you make a mistake when typing an entry, use the Backspace key to correct the entry. Excel does not place the entry in the cell until you press Enter or an arrow key, or click the check mark in the formula bar.

6 Type **February** and press the right-arrow key (→). Then, type **March** and press the right-arrow key (→). Cell E3 is the active cell.

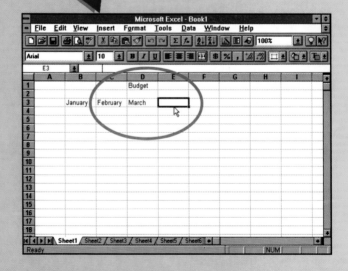

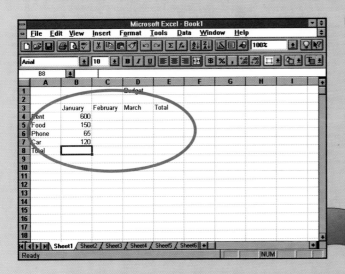

7 Type **Total** and press **Enter**. Then, starting in cell A4, type the remaining data that appears in the figure so that your computer screen matches the screen in the book.

8 Click cell **E1** and type **12-Sep**. Note the check mark in the formula bar. Now click the check mark in the formula bar. Clicking the check mark in the formula bar accepts the entry, enters the date in the cell, and makes E1 remain the active cell.

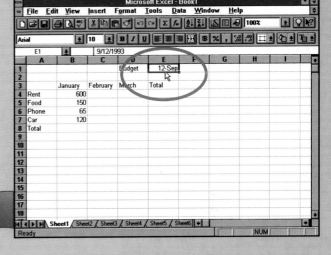

NOTE ▼

In the cell, the date appears as 12-Sep, but Excel stores the date in a different format. In the formula bar, you see 9/12/1993. Notice that the date is right-aligned.

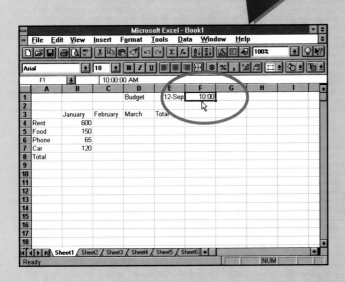

9 Click cell **F1** and type **10:00**. Note the check mark in the formula bar. Now click the check mark in the formula bar. Clicking the check mark in the formula bar accepts the entry, enters the time in the cell, and makes F1 remain the active cell.

NOTE ▼

In the cell, the time appears as 10:00, but the time is stored in a different format. In the formula bar, you see 10:00:00 AM. Notice that the time is right-aligned.

TASK 10

Using Undo

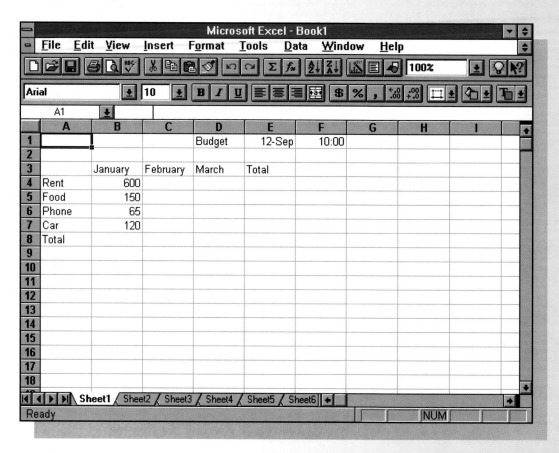

"Why would I do this?"

The Undo feature recovers the most recent changes to worksheet data. For instance, if you edit the worksheet and make a mistake, you can use Undo to reverse the last editing command you performed. Undo becomes very helpful when you need to correct editing and formatting mistakes, especially when you delete data that you did not intend to delete.

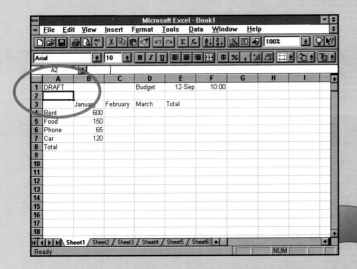

1 Click cell **A1**, type **DRAFT**, and press **Enter**. This step enters the label into cell A1. This is the entry you want to remove with Undo.

2 Click the **Undo** button on the Standard toolbar. Clicking the Undo button selects the Undo command. Excel removes the entry in cell A1. As you can see, the worksheet returns to its preceding form.

WHY WORRY?

Click the Undo button a second time on the Standard toolbar to "undo" the Undo.

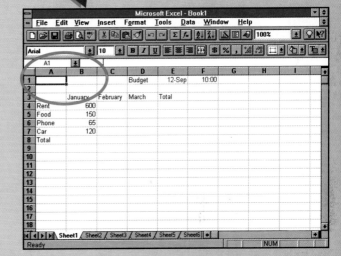

TASK 11

Overwriting a Cell

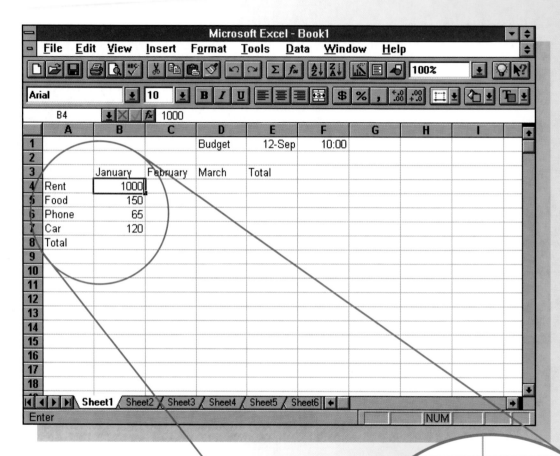

"Why would I do this?"

Overwriting a cell means replacing the existing contents of a cell with new data. If the change is minor, you can edit the cell instead.

Overwriting a cell is handy when you want to correct typing errors or when a cell contains the wrong data. Another reason you might want to overwrite a cell is when you want to play "what if" scenarios.

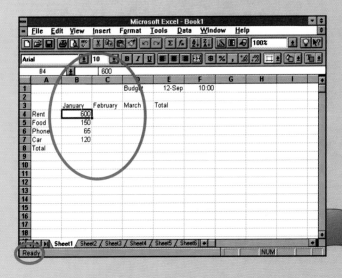

1 Click cell **B4**. This step makes B4 the active cell. The formula bar displays the current entry—the entry you want to overwrite. The mode indicator displays Ready.

2 Type **1000**. 1000 is the new entry and appears in the formula bar.

NOTE ▼

Be careful not to overwrite formulas with labels or values if that is not what you intended. If you overwrite a formula with a value, Excel no longer updates the formula.

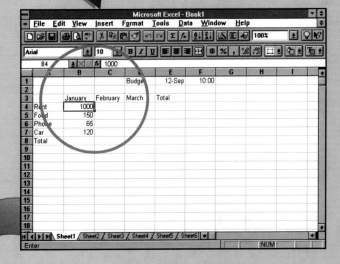

3 Press **Enter**. Pressing Enter replaces the previous entry with the new entry. Excel makes B5 the active cell. Before you press Enter, you can press the Esc key to cancel the changes.

WHY WORRY?

If you make a mistake when typing the entry, use the Backspace key to correct the entry. Excel does not place the entry in the cell until you press Enter or an arrow key.

Editing a Cell

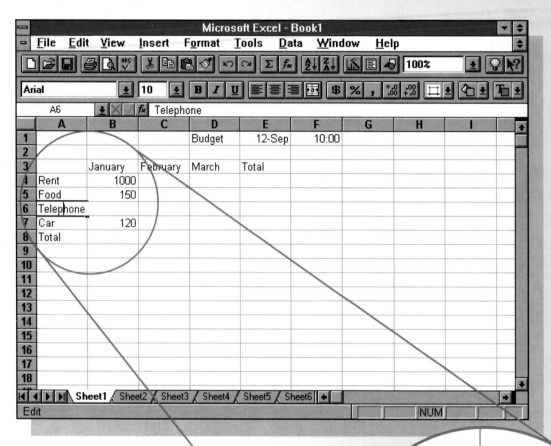

"Why would I do this?"

By editing a cell, you can correct data after it is placed in a cell. You can make changes to part of or all the information in a cell.

Once you know how to edit your data, you won't have to type an entire entry over again. You can just make a few quick changes to correct the contents of a cell. If the new entry is entirely different, then overwrite the entry instead.

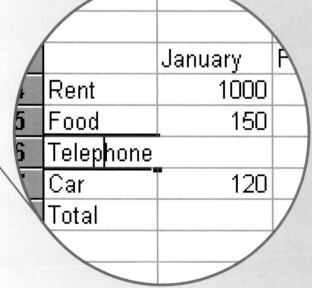

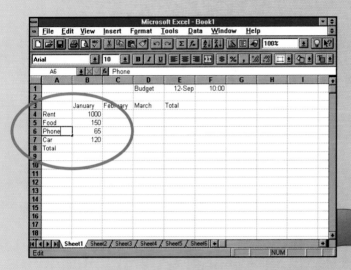

1 Double-click cell **A6**. Double-clicking a cell displays the insertion point at the end of the cell entry—the entry you want to change. Notice that the X and check mark appear in the formula bar.

2 Press **Home**. Pressing the Home key moves the insertion point to the beginning of the entry.

> **NOTE** ▼
>
> You can use the arrow keys to move the insertion point to the characters you want to change or delete.

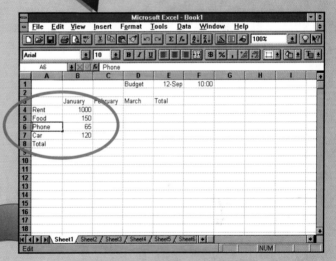

3 Type **Tele**. Typing in Edit mode inserts characters. This entry changes the row label from Phone to TelePhone. Next, we will change the capital P to a lowercase p.

Task 12: Editing a Cell

4 Press **Ins**. Pressing the Ins key in Edit mode lets you overwrite characters. This step highlights the letter P (the character that the insertion point is on) and displays the indicator OVR on the right side of the status bar. This indicator stands for OVERTYPE.

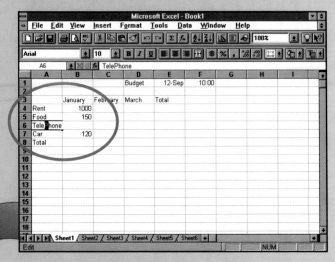

5 Type **p**. This entry changes the capital P to a lowercase p.

NOTE ▼

Before you press Enter to accept the entry, you can press the Esc key or click the X in the formula bar to cancel the changes.

6 Press **Enter**. Pressing Enter accepts the new entry and makes A7 the active cell.

WHY WORRY?

If you make a mistake when typing the entry in Edit mode, use the Del key or the Backspace key to correct the entry. Excel does not place the entry in the cell until you press Enter or an arrow key.

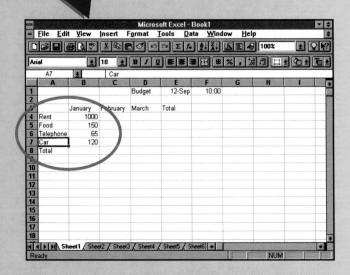

Erasing a Cell

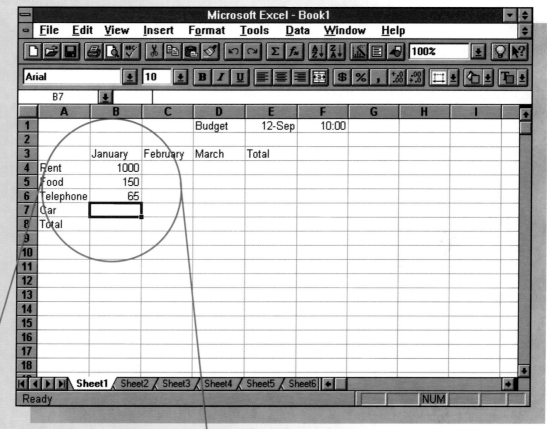

"Why would I do this?"

You can easily erase the contents of a cell by using the Del key. Erasing a cell is useful when you change your mind about the contents after you press Enter to enter the data in the cell. Sometimes you may find that a piece of data you initially typed into a cell is incorrect and needs to be changed. Instead of editing the cell to remove the entry, you can erase the cell with the Del key.

Task 13: Erasing a Cell

1 Select cell **B7**. B7 becomes the active cell. The formula bar displays the current entry—the entry you want to erase.

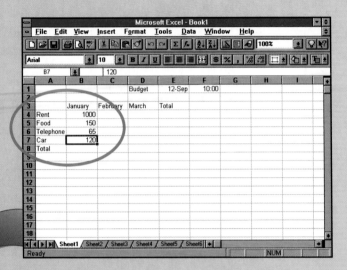

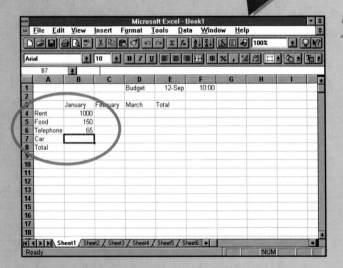

2 Press **Del**. When you press the Del key, Excel deletes the entry in the cell, but leaves the formatting.

NOTE ▼

You can also use the Del key to delete data in a range of cells.

WHY WORRY?

To restore the entry just deleted, click the Undo button on the Standard toolbar.

Copying a Cell

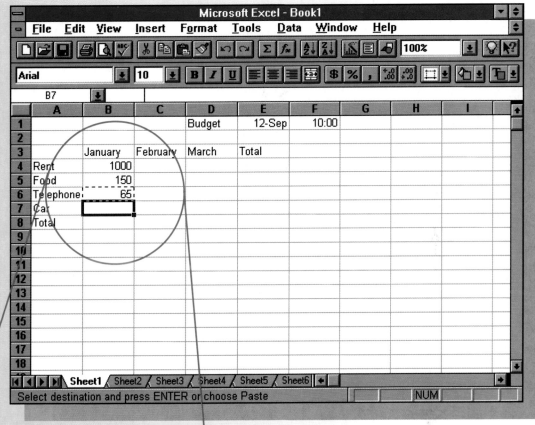

"Why would I do this?"

You can save the time of retyping information on the worksheet by copying a cell over and over again. For example, you might want to copy a label from one cell to another cell. That way you won't have to type the label over again, saving you time and keystrokes.

Task 14: Copying a Cell

1 Select cell **B6**. B6 becomes the active cell. The formula bar displays the current entry—the entry you want to copy.

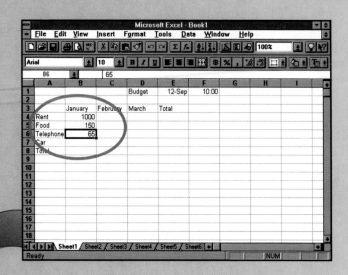

2 Click the **Copy** button on the Standard toolbar. A dashed "marquee" surrounds the cell you are copying. The status bar reminds you how to complete the task: `Select destination and press ENTER or choose Paste.`

3 Select cell **B7**. This step makes B7 the active cell. This cell is where you want the copy to appear.

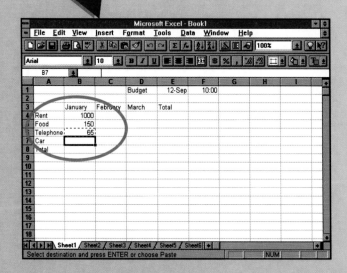

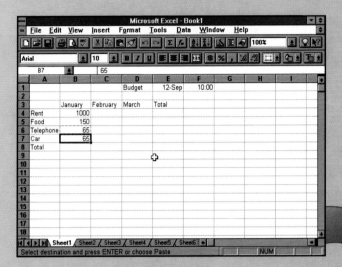

4 Click the **Paste** button on the Standard toolbar. Clicking the Paste button pastes a copy of the data into the cell. As you can see, the entry appears in cell B7.

NOTE ▼

You can also use the Ctrl+C and Ctrl+V key combinations to select the Copy and Paste commands.

5 Press **Esc** to remove the copy marquee in cell B7. Excel copies the entry *and* the format (alignment, protection settings, and so on).

WHY WORRY?

If you copied the wrong data or copied the data to the wrong location, click the Undo button on the Standard toolbar to undo the most recent copy. Then start over.

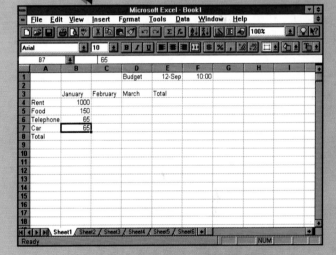

Moving a Cell

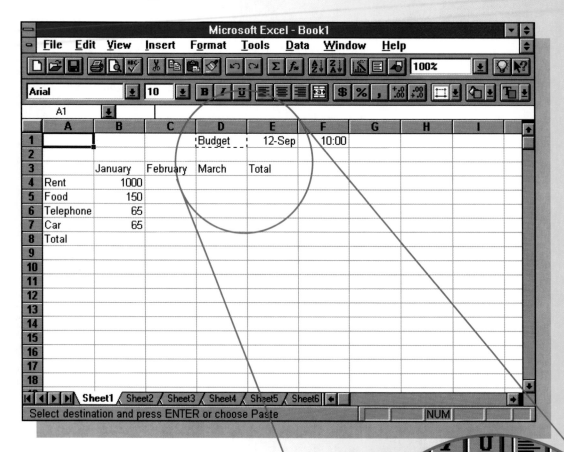

"Why would I do this?"

Excel's Move command lets you remove information from one cell and place it into another cell. You do not have to go to the new cell and enter the same data and then erase the data in the old location.

For example, you might want to move a title that is in the wrong cell or you might want to move data in a worksheet because the layout of the worksheet has changed.

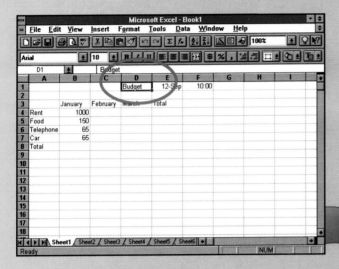

1 Select cell **D1**. D1 becomes the active cell. The formula bar displays the current entry—the entry you want to move.

2 Click the **Cut** button in the Standard toolbar. Clicking the Cut button cuts the entry. A dashed marquee surrounds the cell you are cutting. The status bar reminds you how to complete the task: Select destination and press ENTER or choose Paste.

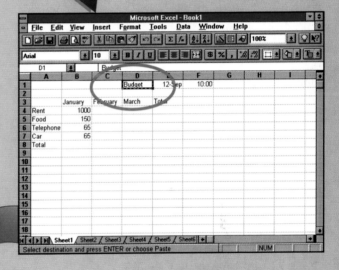

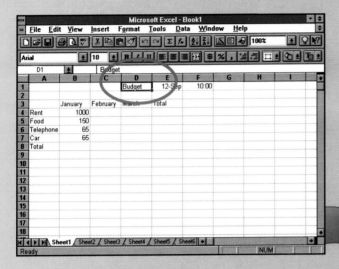

3 Select cell **A1**. This step makes A1 the active cell. This cell is where you want the entry to appear.

Task 15: Moving a Cell

4 Click the **Paste** button (the button that contains a piece of paper on top of a clipboard) on the Standard toolbar to paste the data into the cell. The entry appears in cell A1. Excel moves the entry *and* the format (alignment, protection settings, and so on).

NOTE ▼

You can also use the Ctrl+X and Ctrl+V key combinations to select the Cut and Paste commands.

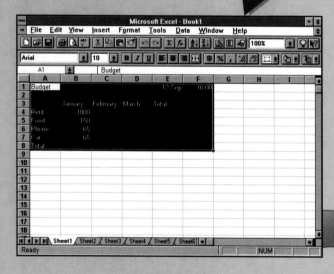

5 Select the range **A1** to **F8**. This step selects the range A1:F8—the range we want to move.

6 Move the mouse pointer to the selected range's border. The mouse pointer changes to an arrow. Drag the border down to row 9 and to the right into column G. The entire worksheet now appears in the new location.

WHY WORRY?

If you moved the wrong data or moved the data to the wrong location, choose the Edit Undo Paste command to undo the most recent move. Then start over.

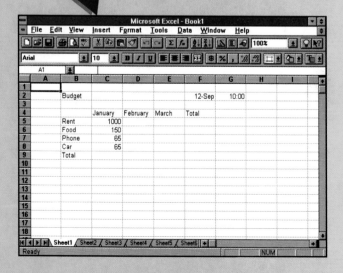

Filling a Range

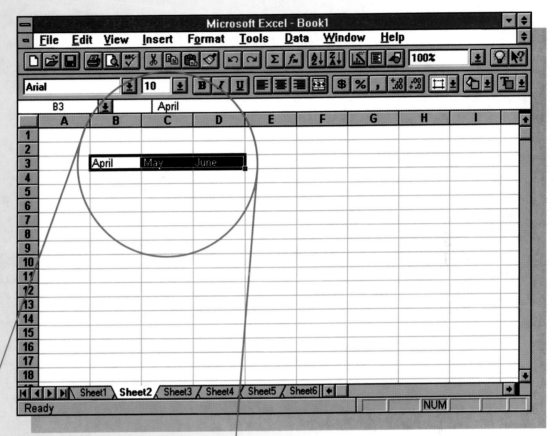

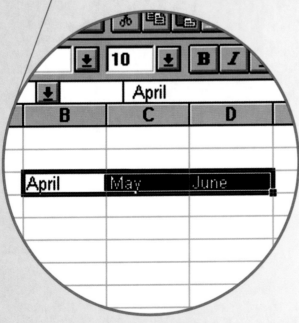

"Why would I do this?"

You can use the Edit Fill Series command to enter a series of numbers or dates. For example, you can type 100 in the first cell in a range. In the second cell type eg, = D1 and click the check mark. Then you can fill in the rest of the range with the numbers 101, 102, 103, and so on.

The Edit Fill Series command is especially useful for entering invoice numbers and ratings. You can also use the Edit Fill Series command to fill a range with the same text, numbers, and formulas.

Task 16: Filling a Range

1 Click the **Sheet2** tab and then click cell **B3**. This step selects Sheet2 and moves this sheet to the top, making it the active sheet. B3 is the active cell where you will enter the first column heading.

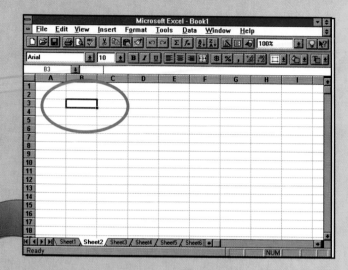

2 Type **April** and click the check mark in the formula bar. This step enters the *start value* for the fill and tells Excel the type of series—in this case, months.

> **NOTE** ▼
>
> Excel will automatically fill the range based on the data in the first cell in the range.

3 Move the mouse pointer to the lower right corner of the current cell's border. The mouse pointer changes to a cross. Drag the cell's border to cells C3 and D3 and release the mouse button. Excel fills the range with months.

> **WHY WORRY?**
>
> To undo the fill series, click the Undo button on the Standard toolbar immediately after filling the range.

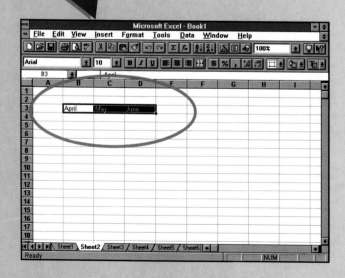

TASK 17

Inserting and Deleting Rows and Columns

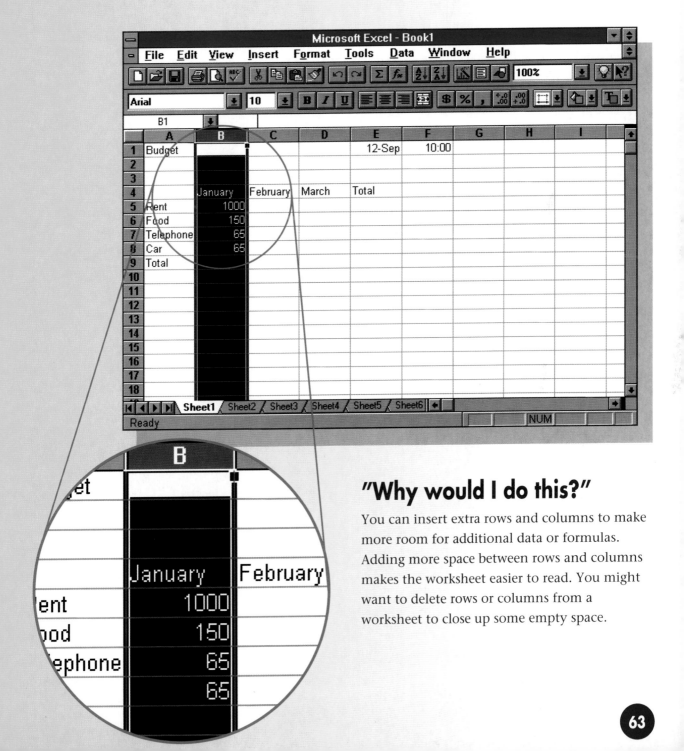

"Why would I do this?"

You can insert extra rows and columns to make more room for additional data or formulas. Adding more space between rows and columns makes the worksheet easier to read. You might want to delete rows or columns from a worksheet to close up some empty space.

Task 17: Inserting and Deleting Rows and Columns

1 Click the **Sheet1** tab, then click cell **C2**. This moves Sheet1 to the top, and selects cell C2. Selecting any cell in a row tells Excel where you want to insert a new row. Excel will insert the new row above row 2.

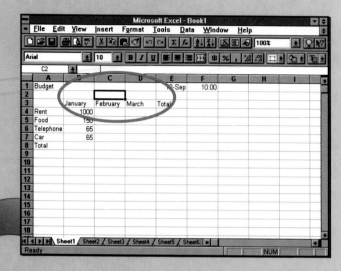

2 Click **Insert** in the menu bar and then click **Rows**. This step selects the Insert Rows command, inserts the new row above row 2, and moves the other rows down. Next—we will delete a column.

3 Click the column header at the top of column B. Be sure to click the column letter, not a cell in the column. This step selects the entire column. Column B is the column you want to delete.

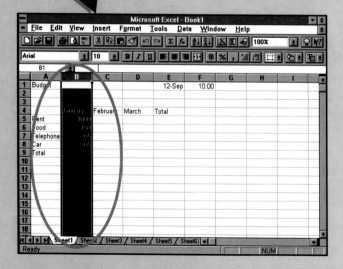

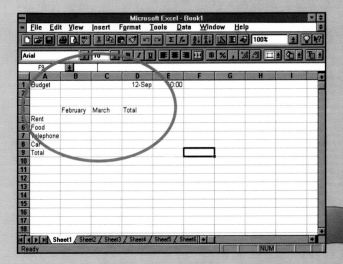

4 Click **Edit** in the menu bar and then click **Delete**. Then click any cell to deselect the range. This step selects the Edit Delete command, deletes the column, and shifts all columns to the right of column B left one column.

NOTE ▼

If you see the Delete dialog box, you did not select the entire column. Click the Entire Column button and then click OK.

5 Click the **Undo** button on the Standard toolbar. Then click any cell to deselect the range. This step restores the deleted column.

WHY WORRY?

To undo a row insertion/deletion or a column insertion/deletion, click the Undo button in the Standard toolbar.

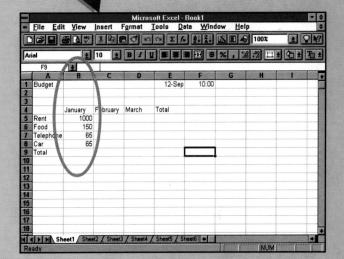

TASK 18
Changing the View

	File	Edit	View	Insert	Format	Tools	Data	Window	Help		
A1				Budget							

	A	B	C	D	E	F	G	H	I	
1	Budget				12-Sep	10:00				
2										
3										
4		January	February	March	Total					
5	Rent	1000								
6	Food	150								
7	Telephone	65								
8	Car	65								
9	Total									
10										
11										
12										
13										
14										
15										
16										
17										
18										
19										
20										
21										
22										
23										
24										

Sheet1 / Sheet2 / Sheet3 / Sheet4 / Sheet5 / Sheet6

"Why would I do this?"

If you want to zoom in and get a closer look
at data in your worksheet, select a higher
percentage of magnification. For instance, if
you enter a label that appears to overlap the
adjacent label, you can inspect this closely
without having to preview or print the
worksheet. If you want to zoom out so the
whole worksheet shows on the screen at one
glance, select a lower percentage of
magnification.

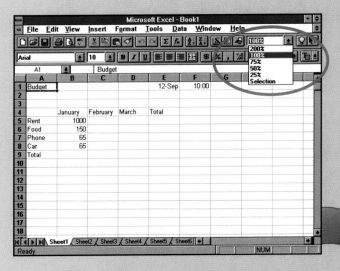

1 Click cell **A1** to reorient the screen. Then click the down arrow next to the Zoom Control box in the Standard toolbar.

2 Now click **200%**. This step enlarges the worksheet to a magnification of 200%.

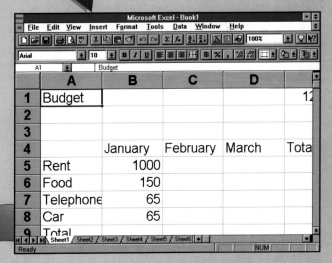

3 Click the down arrow next to the Zoom Control box again. Then click **50%**. This step reduces the worksheet to 50%.

Task 18: Changing the View

4 Click **100%** in the Zoom Control box to restore the worksheet to 100%. Then click **View** in the menu bar, and click **Full Screen**. Note the title bar, toolbars, and status bar no longer display. You can see the full screen display of your worksheet including the menu bar, formula bar, and scroll bars.

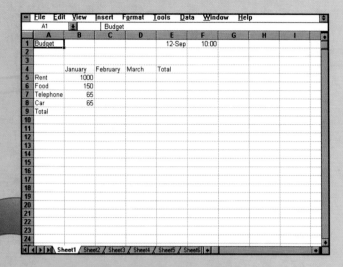

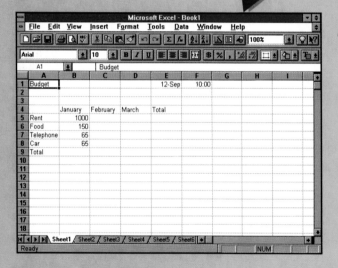

5 Click **View** in the menu bar and then click **Full Screen**. As you can see, Excel redisplays the title bar, toolbars, and status bar.

WHY WORRY?

If you select the wrong magnification percentage, just select a different percentage to switch to the percentage you want.

Freezing Column and Row Titles

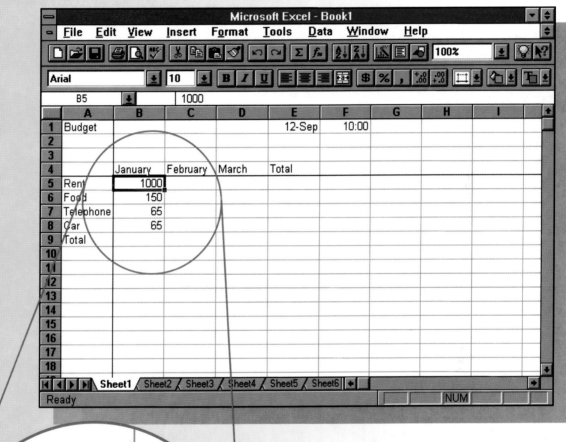

"Why would I do this?"

Often, you will enter data in a worksheet that exceeds more than one screen, requiring you to scroll to the right or down to view other areas use Excel's Window Freeze Panes command to freeze column and row titles so that they remain stationary when you scroll to other parts of the worksheet.

Task 19: Freezing Column and Row Titles

1 Click cell **B5**. Cell B5 is where we want to freeze the titles.

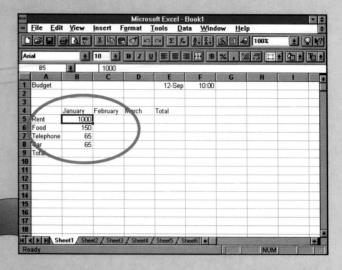

2 Click **Window** in the menu bar and then click **Freeze Panes**. This step splits the window into panes and freezes the titles above and to the left of the cell pointer.

> **NOTE** ▼
>
> A horizontal line splits the window into a top and bottom pane, and a vertical line splits the window into a left and right pane.

3 Drag the scroll box in the horizontal scroll bar to the far right side of the scroll bar. As you can see, the row titles remain on-screen.

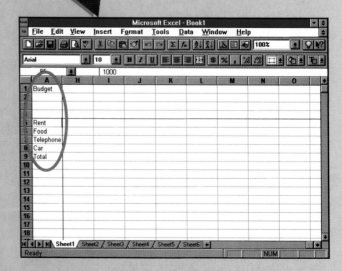

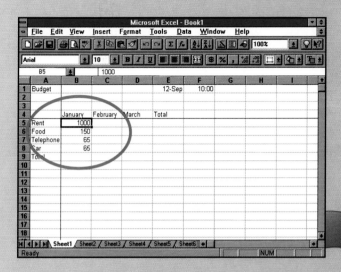

4 Press **Ctrl+Home**. This step returns the cell pointer to the original cell pointer location.

5 Drag the scroll box in the vertical scroll bar down to the bottom of the scroll bar. As you can see, the column titles remain on-screen.

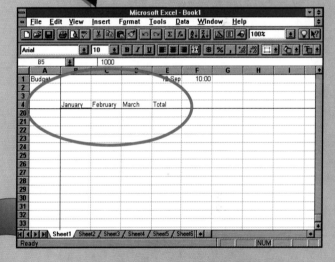

6 Click **Window** in the menu bar and then click **Unfreeze Panes**. Excel restores the worksheet to the original display.

WHY WORRY?

If you freeze the panes in the wrong place, simply select the Window Unfreeze Panes command. Then start over.

Hiding and Displaying Columns and Rows

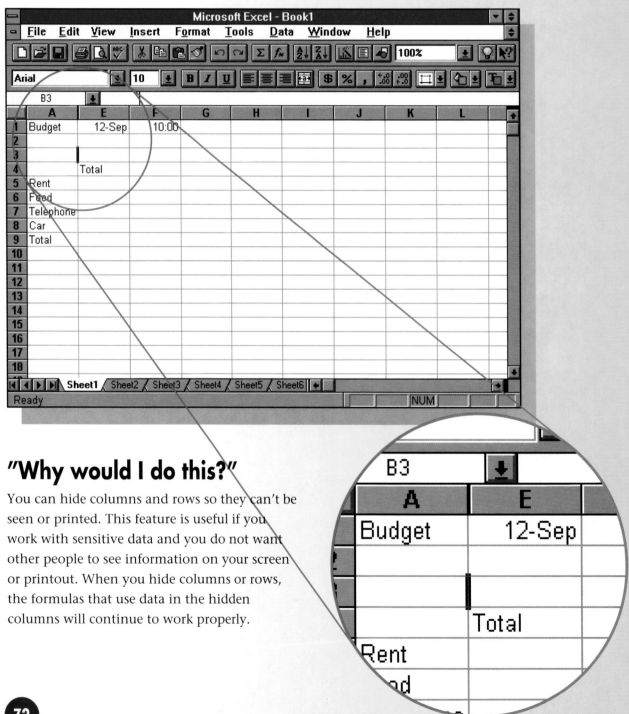

"Why would I do this?"

You can hide columns and rows so they can't be seen or printed. This feature is useful if you work with sensitive data and you do not want other people to see information on your screen or printout. When you hide columns or rows, the formulas that use data in the hidden columns will continue to work properly.

Task 20: Hiding and Displaying Columns and Rows

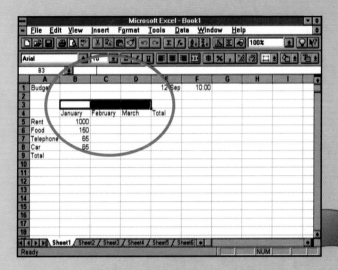

1 Hold down the mouse button and drag the mouse to select cells **B3**, **C3**, and **D3**. This step selects a cell in each column you want to hide—B, C, and D. You can click any cell in the column(s) you want to hide. (You cannot hide only part of a column.)

2 Click **Format** in the menu bar, click **Column**, and then click **Hide**. This step selects the Format Column Hide command. Excel hides the selected columns. You can tell by the column letters (A, E, F) that columns B, C, and D are hidden. Next—we will redisplay the hidden columns.

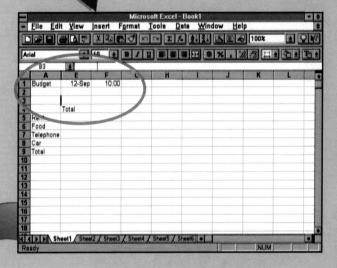

3 Click **Format** in the menu bar, click **Column**, and then click **Unhide**. This step selects the Format Column Unhide command. Excel redisplays the hidden columns.

WHY WORRY?

If you hide the wrong columns, click the Undo button on the Standard toolbar to display the recently hidden columns. Then start over.

Splitting Worksheets

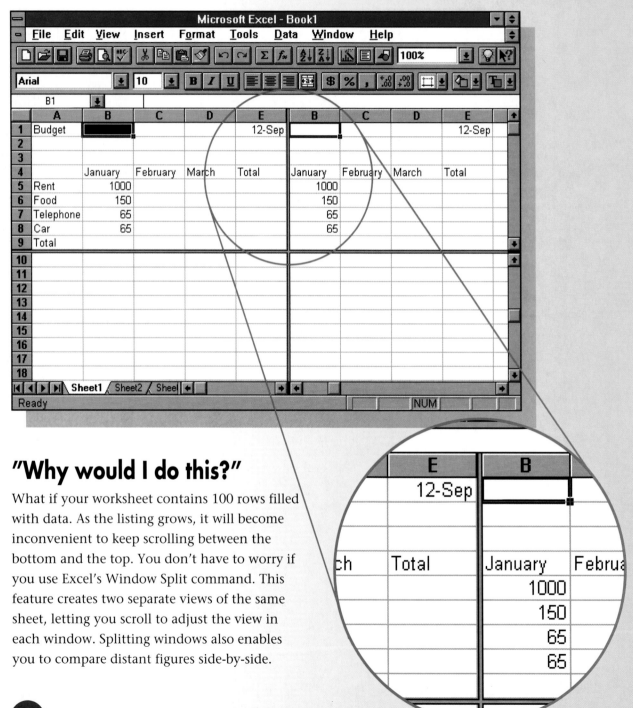

"Why would I do this?"

What if your worksheet contains 100 rows filled with data. As the listing grows, it will become inconvenient to keep scrolling between the bottom and the top. You don't have to worry if you use Excel's Window Split command. This feature creates two separate views of the same sheet, letting you scroll to adjust the view in each window. Splitting windows also enables you to compare distant figures side-by-side.

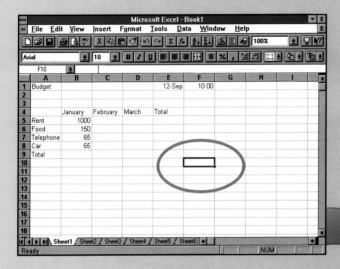

1 Click cell **F10**. F10 is the cell where you want to split the worksheet window.

2 Click **Window** in the menu bar and then click **Split**. This step splits the window horizontally into four panes. Notice there are two vertical scroll bars along the right side of the worksheet and two horizontal scroll bars across the bottom of the worksheet.

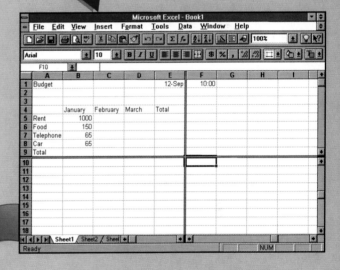

3 Press **F6** three times. Pressing the F6 (Window) key moves the cell pointer to the next window clockwise. The cell pointer appears in the top right pane.

NOTE ▼

Press Shift+F6 to move the cell pointer to the previous window counter-clockwise.

75

Task 21: Splitting Worksheets

4 Press the left-arrow key (←) four times. This step shows you how to scroll in a window pane. Now you can compare the January figures in the top right pane to the totals in the top left pane.

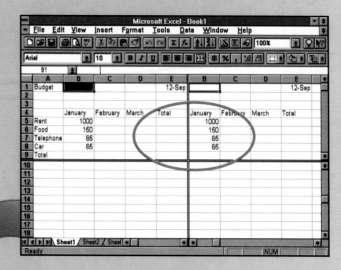

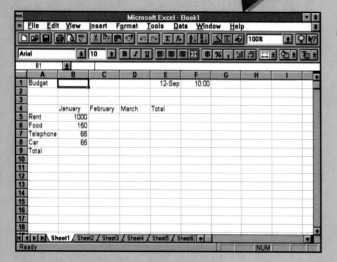

5 Click **Window** in the menu bar and then click **Remove Split**. This step restores the window to the original display.

WHY WORRY?

If you split the worksheet in the wrong place, simply select the Window Remove Split command. Then start over.

Sorting Data

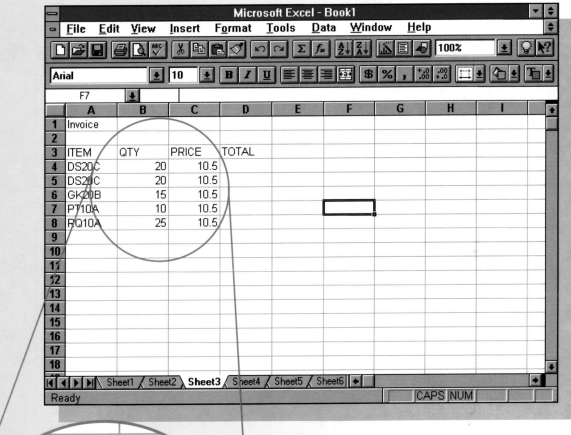

"Why would I do this?"

Excel's Sort feature lets you sort text in alphabetical order and numbers in numeric order. The text and numbers can be sorted in ascending (lowest to highest) or descending (highest to lowest) order.

You might want to sort a column of row headings so that you can easily look down the sorted column to find the information you want.

Task 22: Sorting Data

1 Click the **Sheet3** tab. Starting in cell A1, type the data that appears in the figure so that your computer screen matches the screen in the book.

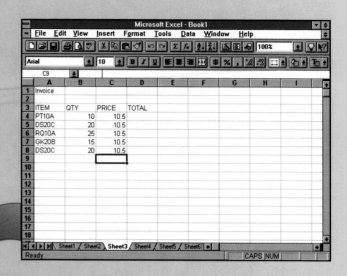

NOTE ▼

Keep in mind that you can sort by any column, sort more than one column, and sort in descending order. For complete information on these options, see your Microsoft Excel documentation.

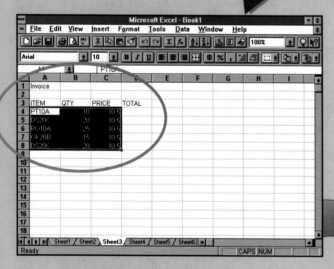

2 Hold down the mouse button and drag the mouse to select the range **A4:C8**. Be sure to select all the data in the rows; otherwise, the entries will be mismatched. Be sure *not* to select the column headings.

NOTE ▼

You can also select A4:C8 by selecting cell A4, holding down the Shift key, and moving the cell pointer to cell C8.

3 Click the **Sort Ascending** button on the Standard toolbar (the button with A on top of Z beside a down arrow). Then click any cell to deselect the range. Excel sorts the data in alphabetical order according to the item names.

WHY WORRY?

If the sort does not work as you planned, immediately select the Edit Undo Sort command to restore the range to its original order. Then, click any cell to deselect the range.

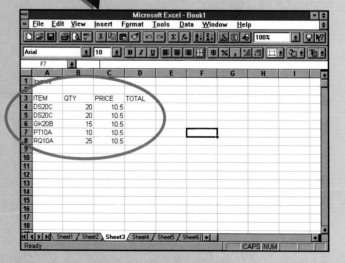

Finding and Replacing Data

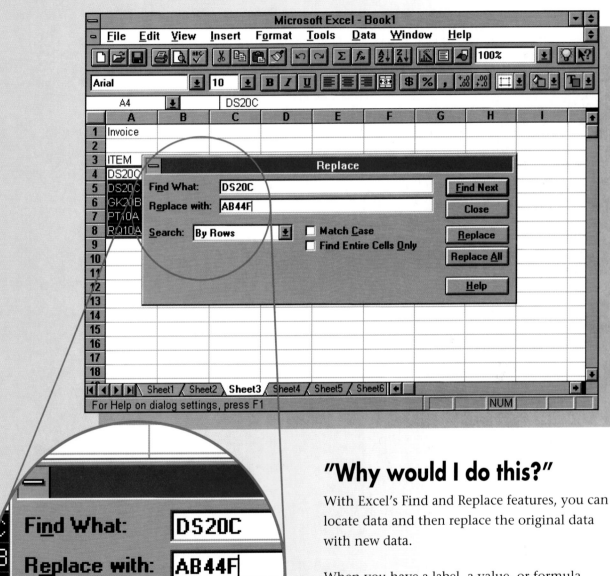

"Why would I do this?"

With Excel's Find and Replace features, you can locate data and then replace the original data with new data.

When you have a label, a value, or formula that is entered incorrectly throughout the worksheet, you can use the Edit Replace command to search and replace all occurrences of the incorrect information with the correct data.

Task 23: Finding and Replacing Data

1 Hold down the mouse button and drag the mouse to select cells **A4** to **A8**. This step selects the range you want to search—A4:A8.

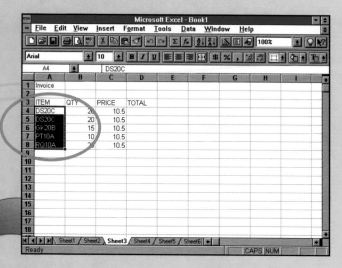

2 Click **Edit** in the menu bar and then click **Replace**. This step selects the Edit Replace command. Excel displays the Replace dialog box. The insertion point is in the Find What text box.

3 Type **DS20C**. *DS20C* is the text you want to find and replace.

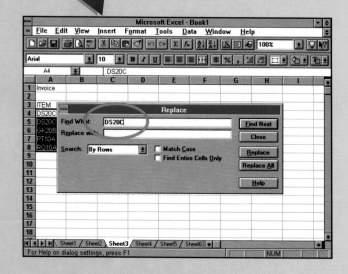

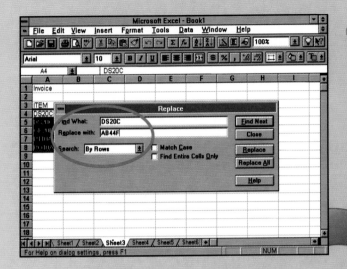

4 Click in the **Replace With** text box or press the Tab key and type **AB44F**. *AB44F* is the new label—the label you want to use as the replacement.

5 Click **Replace All** to begin the search. When Excel finishes replacing all occurrences, click outside the range to deselect it. This step starts the search and tells Excel to replace all occurrences of *DS20C* with *AB44F*.

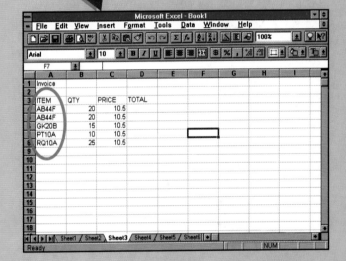

NOTE ▼

Be sure that you want to replace all occurrences before you select the Replace All button. You can also search for and replace one occurrence at a time. See your Microsoft Excel documentation for more information.

WHY WORRY?

To undo the replacements, click the Undo button on the Standard toolbar immediately after replacing the data.

Checking Your Spelling

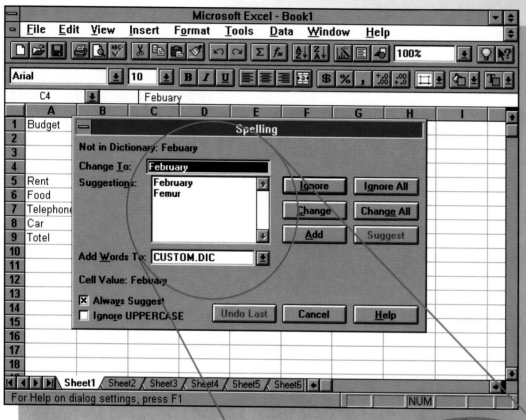

"Why would I do this?"

Excel's spell checker rapidly finds and highlights for correction the misspellings in a worksheet. Spell checking is an important feature that makes your worksheets look professional and letter perfect.

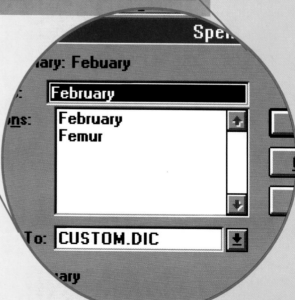

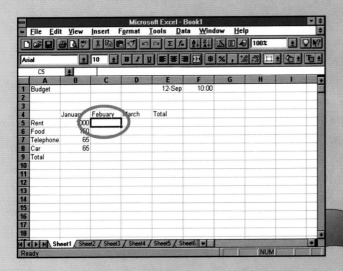

1 Click the **Sheet1** tab. In cell **C4**, remove the first occurrence of the letter r in the word February.

NOTE ▼

Remember, you can double-click a cell to edit it, then press Enter when you're finished.

2 In cell **A9**, change the a in the word Total to an e.

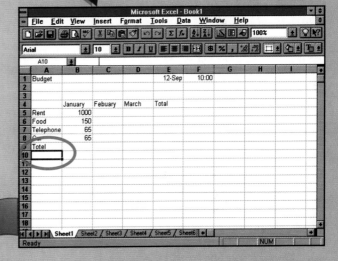

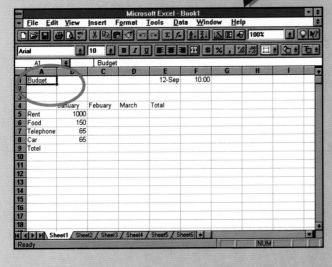

3 Select cell **A1**. This step tells Excel to begin spell checking at the top instead of the middle of the worksheet.

Task 24: Checking Your Spelling

4 To begin the spell checker, click the **Spelling** button on the Standard toolbar (the button with the check mark and *ABC* text). Excel finds the first misspelled word Febuary and displays the word at the top of the Spelling dialog box. The correct word February appears in the Change To box and in the suggestions list.

> **NOTE** ▼
>
> The Spelling dialog box lists suggested spellings for the word not found in the dictionary.

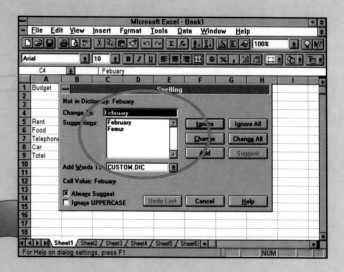

5 Click **Change**. This step replaces the incorrect word with the correct word in the worksheet. The spell checker finds the next misspelled word Totel and displays the word at the top of the Spelling dialog box.

> **NOTE** ▼
>
> The Spelling dialog box covers up the change in the worksheet, but you can see the change when the spell checking is complete and the dialog box is closed.

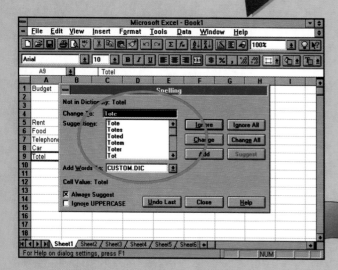

6 Click the down scroll arrow in the Suggestions list to find the correct word. When you see the word Total, click it. This step selects the word and displays it in the Change To box.

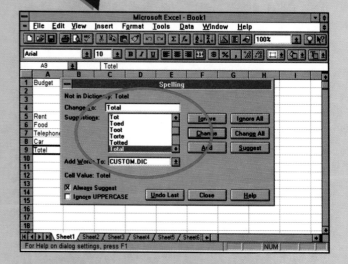

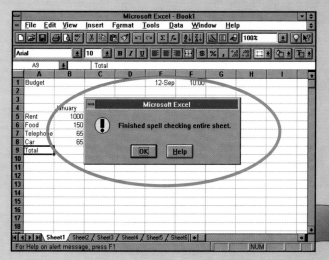

7 Click **Change**. This step replaces the incorrect word with the correct word in the worksheet. The spell checker doesn't find any more misspelled words and displays the prompt: Finished spell checking entire sheet.

8 Click **OK**. This confirms that spell checking is complete. Now you can see the corrected spelling error in February in cell C4, and Total in cell A9.

WHY WORRY?

If you mistakenly select the wrong Spell option, you can click the Undo Last button in the Spelling dialog box to undo the last option you chose or you can correct the mistake after you exit the spell checker.

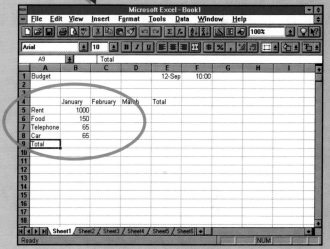

PART III

Working with Formulas

Part III: Working with Formulas

In Part II you learned how to enter data and change your worksheet data using various editing techniques. This section shows you how to add, subtract, multiply, and divide data with formulas. You also learn how to total cells with the SUM function, calculate an average, copy a formula, and assign an English name to a range of cells.

$$E=mc^2$$

Formulas calculate the values in other cells of the worksheet. Once you enter a formula, you can change the values in the referenced cells, and Excel automatically recalculates its value based on the cell changes. You can include any cells in your formula. The cells do not have to be next to each other. Also, you can combine mathematical operations—for example, C3+C4–D5.

Functions are abbreviated formulas that perform a specific operation on a group of values. Excel provides over 250 functions that can help you with tasks ranging from determining loan payments to calculating investment returns.

The SUM function is a shortcut for entering an addition formula. SUM is the name of the function that automatically sums entries in a range. You enter the range within parentheses. For example, first you type **=SUM(**. You can type the function in lower- or uppercase letters. Then you select the range. A dashed border called a marquee surrounds the selected range. Finally, you enclose the function with a parenthesis. Typing **)** tells Excel that you are finished selecting the range. Excel inserts the range coordinates in the parentheses. Alternatively, you can type Alt+ = to create a SUM formula. This section shows you how to use the AutoSum button in the Standard toolbar to create a sum formula.

The AVERAGE function is a predefined formula that adds the values you specify in a range and then divides the sum by the number of values in the range. You can use the Function Wizard button (*fx*) in the formula bar to enter the AVERAGE function in the formula instead of typing the word "average." You can also use the Function Wizard button in the Standard toolbar to create a function.

For information on creating complex formulas, the order of precedence (the order in which Excel evaluates formulas), and functions, refer to your Microsoft Excel documentation.

Excel's Copy command lets you copy formulas and place them in the appropriate cells. You do not have to go to each cell and enter the same formula. You can also copy one cell to another cell, and you can copy one cell to a range of cells. You learn how to use the Copy and Paste buttons to copy a formula. You also use the fill handle to copy a formula to a range of cells.

In Excel, there are three types of cell references: relative, absolute, and mixed. The type of cell reference you use in a formula determines how the formula is affected when you copy the formula into a different cell. The formulas you create in this section contain *relative cell references*. This means that when you copy a formula from one cell to another, the cell references in the formula change to reflect the cells at the new location of the formula.

An *absolute cell reference* is an entry in a formula that does not refer to a new cell when the formula is copied to a new cell. There are certain formulas you might want to create in which you want an entry to always refer to one specific cell value. For example, you might want to calculate the interest on several different principal amounts. The interest percentage remains unchanged, or absolute, so the entry in the formula that refers to the interest percentage is designated as an absolute cell reference. The principal amounts change, so they have relative cell reference entries in the formula. When you copy this absolute formula, the interest cell reference always refers to the one cell that contains the interest percentage.

A *mixed cell reference* is a single cell entry in a formula that contains both a relative and an absolute cell reference. A mixed cell reference is helpful when you need a formula that always refers to the values in a specific column, but the values in the rows must change, and vice versa.

Excel's Name command lets you assign an English name to a value or a formula in a single cell or a range of cells. You can then use the assigned name rather than the cell addresses when specifying a cell or range of cells for use in copying, moving, erasing, formatting, or printing. The cell addresses in a range are simply locations and do not describe the range itself. Defining range names provides you with a more meaningful way of specifying ranges.

Formulas can be as simple or as complex as necessary to get the job done. In this section, the calculations are restricted to the more basic mathematical formulas you work with on a daily basis. The capability of entering formulas in worksheets shows you much of the power and convenience of programs like Excel.

Adding Data with a Formula

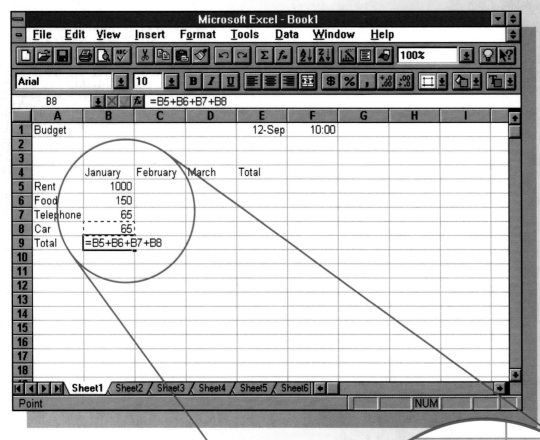

"Why would I do this?"

In your budget, you could just add the values in the cells, but if you change any of the values, the sum is not current. Because a formula references the cells rather than the values, Excel updates the sum whenever you change the values in the cells. In an expense report, you might want to enter a formula to sum your expenses. You also can use the SUM function to add values.

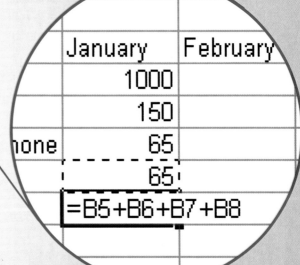

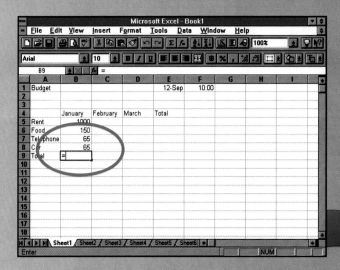

1 Click cell **B9**. This cell is where the result of the formula appears. Type =.

> **NOTE** ▼
>
> Typing = tells Excel that you want to create a formula. You then select the cells you want to include in this formula.

2 Click cell **B5**. Cell B5 is the first cell you want to include in the addition formula. Excel surrounds the cell with a dashed marquee. You see =B5 in the formula bar and in cell B9.

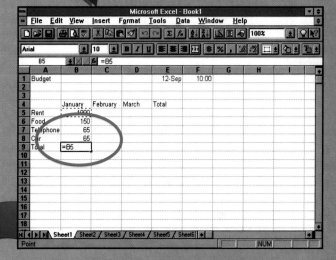

3 Type +. The + sign is the operator. It tells Excel which mathematical operation you want to perform—in this case, addition. You see =B5+ in the formula bar and in cell B9. The cell pointer returns to B9.

Task 25: Adding Data with a Formula

4 Click cell **B6**. Cell B6 is the second cell you want to include in the addition formula. A dashed marquee surrounds the cell. You see **=B5+B6** in the formula bar and in cell B9.

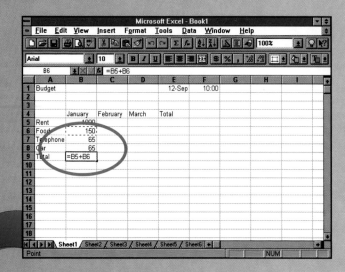

5 Type **+**. The + sign is the operator. It tells Excel which mathematical operation you want to perform—in this case, addition. You see **=B5+B6+** in the formula bar and in cell B9. The cell pointer returns to B9.

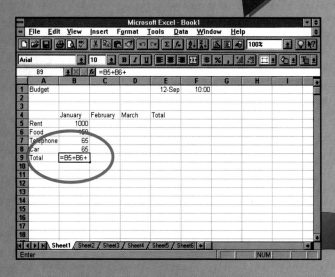

6 Select cell **B7**. Cell B7 is the third cell you want to include in the addition formula. A dashed box surrounds the cell. You see **=B5+B6+B7** in the formula bar and in cell B9.

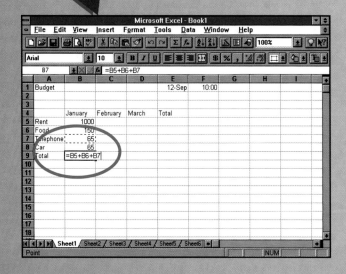

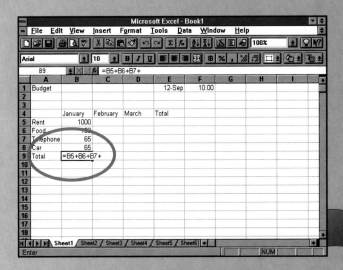

7 Type +. The + sign is the operator. It tells Excel which mathematical operation you want to perform—in this case, addition. You see =B5+B6+B7+ in the formula bar and in cell B9. The cell pointer returns to cell B9.

8 Select cell **B8**. Cell B8 is the last cell you want to include in the addition formula. A dashed box surrounds the cell. You see =B5+B6+B7+B8 in the formula bar and in cell B9.

WHY WORRY?

To delete the most recent entry, click the Undo button on the Standard toolbar immediately after entering the addition formula.

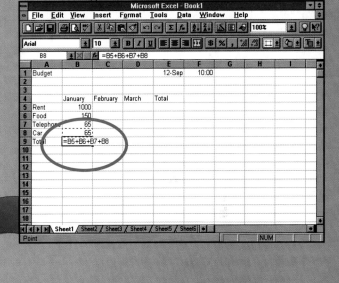

9 Press **Enter**. Pressing Enter tells Excel that you are finished creating the formula. You see the result of the formula (1280) in cell B9. Whenever B9 is the active cell, the formula =B5+B6+B7+B8 appears in the formula bar.

NOTE ▼

If you see number signs (#) in the column, the entry is too long. You must change the column width.

Subtracting Data with a Formula

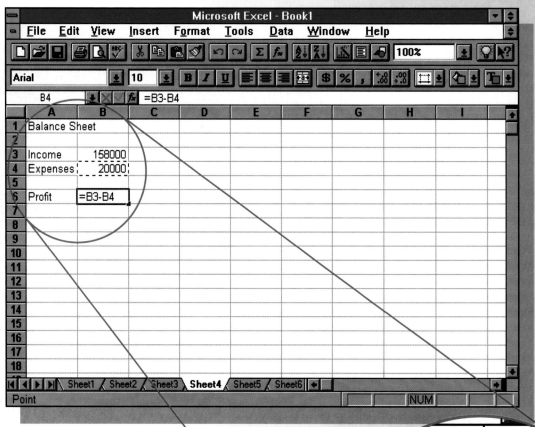

"Why would I do this?"

You could just subtract the values in the cells, but if you change any of the values, the result is not current. Because a formula references the cells rather than the values, Excel updates the result whenever you change the values in the cells. For example, you might want to enter a formula to subtract expenses from income to calculate profit. To learn how to enter a subtraction formula, create a balance sheet on Sheet4.

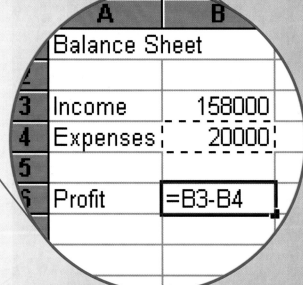

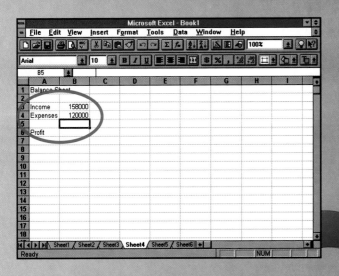

1 Click the **Sheet4** tab to move to Sheet4. Starting in cell A1, type the data that appears in the figure so that your computer screen matches the screen in the book.

2 Click cell **B6**. This cell is where the result of the formula appears. Type =.

> **NOTE** ▼
>
> Typing = tells Excel that you want to create a formula. You then select the cells you want to include in this formula.

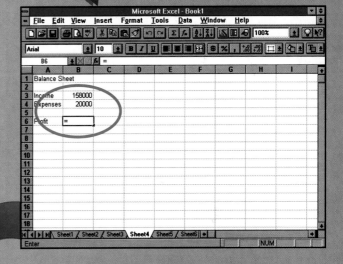

3 Select cell **B3**. Cell B3 is the first cell you want to include in the subtraction formula. Excel surrounds the cell with a dashed marquee. You see =B3 in the formula bar and in cell B6.

Task 26: Subtracting Data with a Formula

4 Type –. The – sign is the operator. It tells Excel which mathematical operation you want to perform—in this case, subtraction. You see =B3 - in the formula bar and in cell B6. The cell pointer returns to B6.

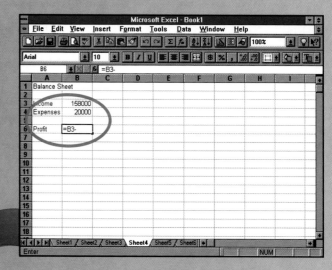

5 Select cell **B4**. Cell B4 is the second cell you want to include in the subtraction formula. A dashed box surrounds the cell. You see =B3 - B4 in the formula bar and in cell B6.

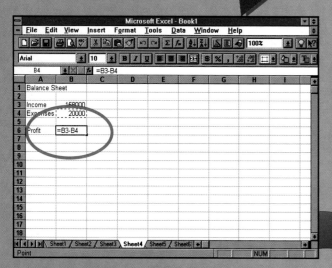

WHY WORRY?

To delete the most recent entry, click the Undo button in the Standard toolbar immediately after entering the subtraction formula.

6 Press **Enter**. Pressing Enter tells Excel that you are finished creating the formula. You see the result of the formula (138000) in cell B6. Whenever B6 is the active cell, the formula =B3 - B4 appears in the formula bar.

NOTE ▼

If you see number signs (#) in the column, the entry is too long. You must change the column width.

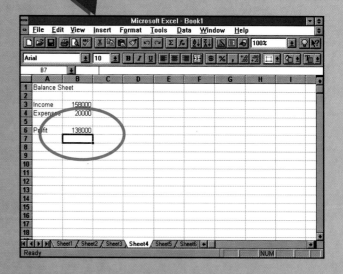

Multiplying Data with a Formula

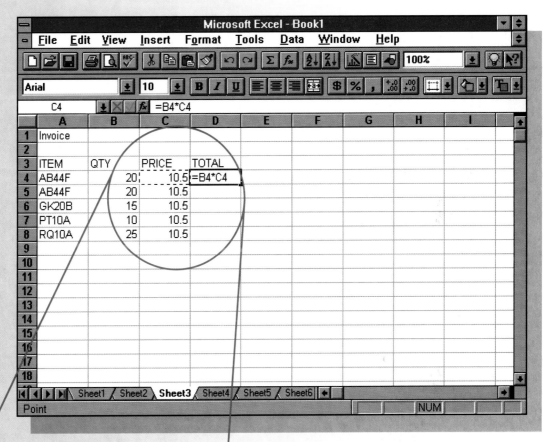

"Why would I do this?"

In your invoice, you could just multiply the values in the cells (20*10.5), but if you change any of the values, the result is not current. Because a formula references the cells (B4 and C4) rather than the values, Excel updates the result whenever you change the values in the cells. For example, you might want to enter a formula to multiply the quantity by the price to calculate the total price.

Task 27: Multiplying Data with a Formula

1 Click the **Sheet3** tab to move to the invoice on Sheet3. Then click cell **D4**. This cell is where the result of the formula appears.

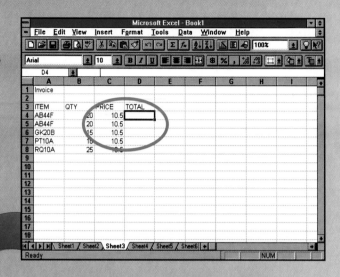

2 Type =.

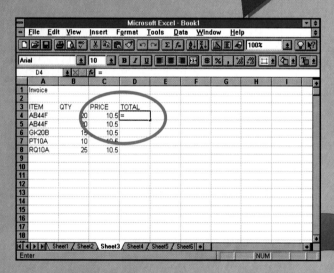

3 Select cell **B4**. Cell B4 is the first cell you want to include in the formula. A dashed marquee surrounds the cell. You see =B4 in the formula bar and in cell D4.

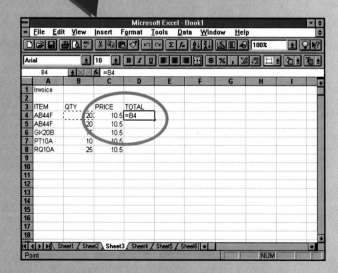

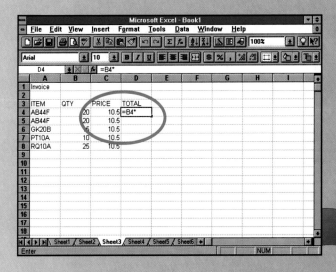

4 Type *. The * sign is the operator. It tells Excel which mathematical operation you want to perform—in this case, multiplication. You see =B4* in the formula bar and in cell D4. The cell pointer returns to D4.

5 Select cell **C4**. Cell C4 is the second cell you want to include in the formula. You see =B4*C4 in the formula bar and in cell D4.

WHY WORRY?

To delete the most recent entry, click the Undo button in the Standard toolbar immediately after entering the multiplication formula.

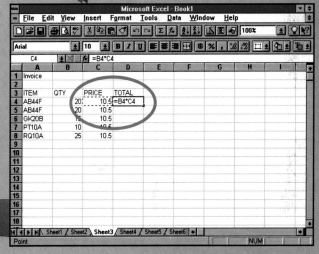

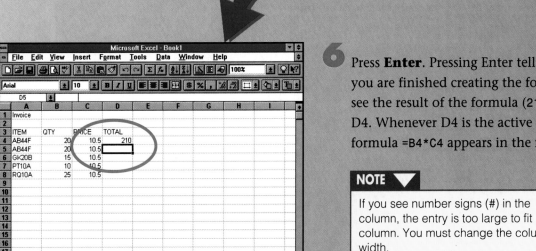

6 Press **Enter**. Pressing Enter tells Excel that you are finished creating the formula. You see the result of the formula (210) in cell D4. Whenever D4 is the active cell, the formula =B4*C4 appears in the formula bar.

NOTE ▼

If you see number signs (#) in the column, the entry is too large to fit in the column. You must change the column width.

Dividing Data with a Formula

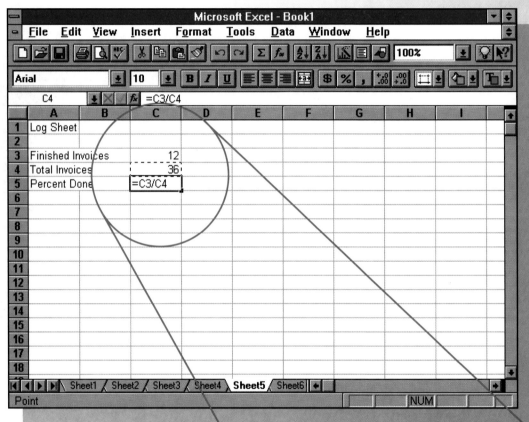

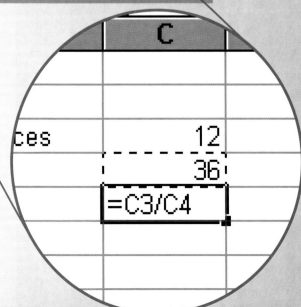

"Why would I do this?"

You could just divide the values in the cells, but if you change any of the values, the result is not current. Because a formula references the cells rather than the values, Excel updates the result whenever you change the values in the cells. You might want to enter a division formula to calculate a percentage of the total.

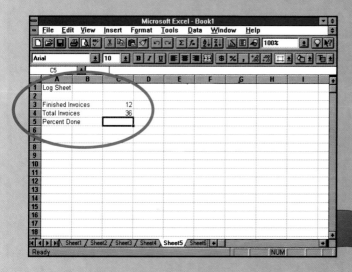

1 Click the **Sheet5** tab to move to Sheet5. Starting in cell A1, type the data that appears in the figure so that your computer screen matches the screen in the book.

2 Click cell **C5**. This cell is where the result of the formula appears. Type =.

NOTE ▼

> Typing = tells Excel that you want to create a formula. You then select the cells you want to include in the formula.

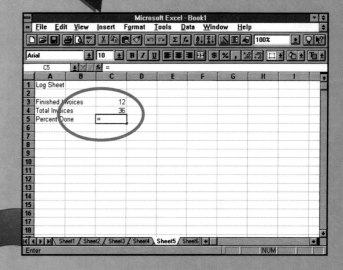

3 Select cell **C3**. Cell C3 is the first cell you want to include in the formula. A dashed marquee surrounds the cell. You see =C3 in the formula bar and in cell C5.

Task 28: Dividing Data with a Formula

4 Type **/**. The / sign is the operator. It tells Excel which mathematical operation you want to perform—in this case, division. The cell pointer returns to C5.

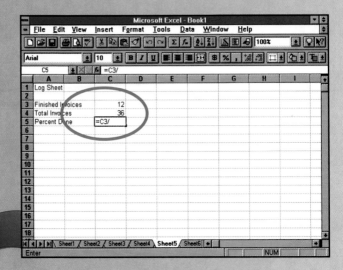

5 Select cell **C4**. Cell C4 is the second cell you want to include in the formula. A dashed marquee surrounds the cell. You see =C3/C4 in the formula bar and in cell C5.

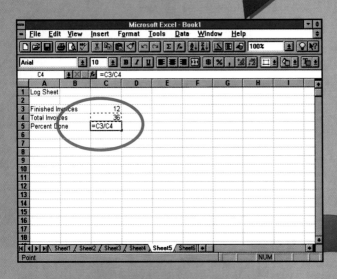

WHY WORRY?

To delete the most recent entry, click the Undo button in the Standard toolbar immediately after entering the division formula.

6 Press **Enter**. Pressing Enter tells Excel that you finished creating the formula. You see the result of the formula (0.333333) in cell C5. Whenever C5 is the active cell, the formula =C3/C4 appears in the formula bar.

NOTE ▼

If you see number signs (#) in the column, the entry is too large to fit in the column. You must change the column width.

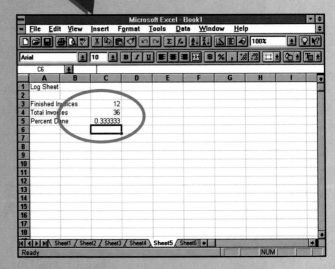

Totaling Cells with the SUM Function

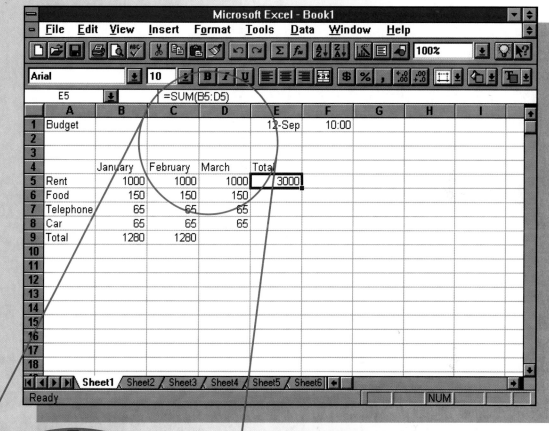

"Why would I do this?"

A function is a predefined formula. You provide the variable parts of the formula, and Excel calculates the result. The SUM function enables you to sum a range. If you later insert or delete rows (or columns), Excel automatically updates the total. For example, you can replace a lengthy column or row total formula with a simple SUM function.

Task 29: Totaling Cells with the SUM Function

1 Click the **Sheet1** tab to move to the budget on Sheet1. Then, select the range **B5:B8** by selecting cell B5 and dragging the mouse down to cell B8. B5:B8 is the range that contains the numbers you use to fill columns C and D.

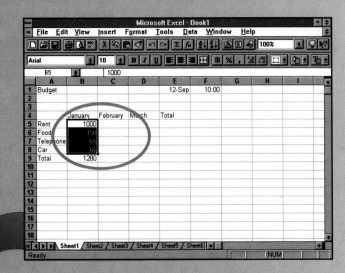

2 Move the mouse pointer to the fill handle in the lower right corner of cell B8 until the mouse pointer changes to a cross. Then drag the selected range across columns C and D. This step fills the range C5:D8 with the numbers from column B.

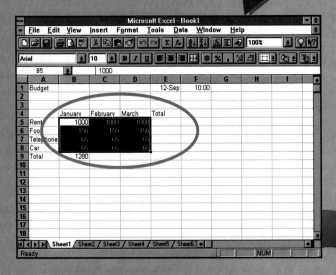

3 Click cell **C9**. C9 is the cell where you want to place the SUM function.

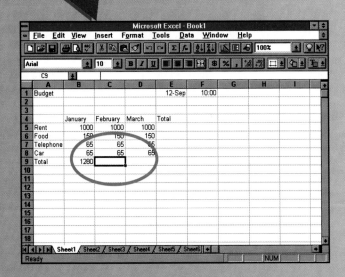

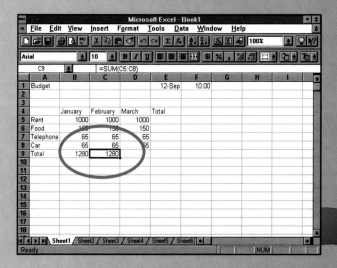

4 Double-click the **AutoSum** button on the Standard toolbar. Double-clicking the AutoSum button enters the SUM function in the formula bar and in the cell. =SUM(C5:C8) appears in the formula bar. You see the result of the formula, 1280, in cell C9. In a later task in this part, you copy this formula into cell D9.

5 Follow steps 3 and 4 to enter the SUM function in cell E5. =SUM(B5:D5) appears in the formula bar. You see the result of the formula, 3000, in cell E5.

WHY WORRY?

To delete the most recent entry, click the Undo button in the Standard toolbar immediately after entering the SUM function.

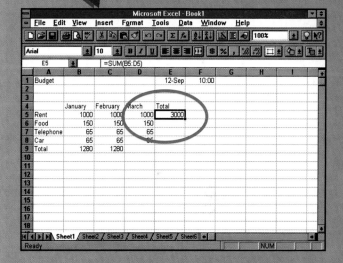

Calculating an Average

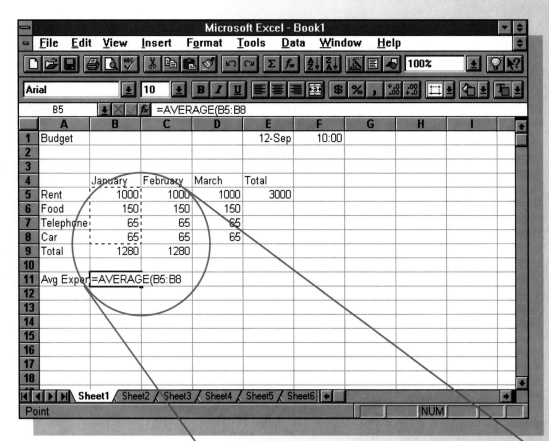

"Why would I do this?"

You can calculate an average by using Excel's AVERAGE function. The AVERAGE function is similar to the SUM function. For example, you can calculate the average expense, income, grade, rating, or salary, and so on.

In the budget, find the average of the total expenses for January. You enter the label Avg Expense in cell A11 and the AVERAGE function in cell B11.

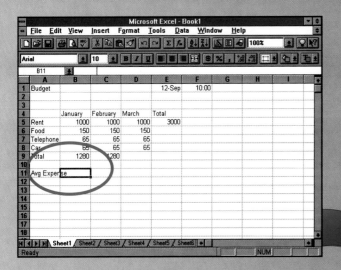

1 Click cell **A11**, type **Avg Expense**, and press the right-arrow key (→). B11 is the cell in which you want to place the formula that calculates an average.

NOTE ▼

Notice that the long label spills into cell B11. You can widen column A to accommodate the long entry.

2 Type **=AVERAGE(**. AVERAGE is the name of the function that automatically averages entries in a range. You enter the range that you want to average within the parentheses. (You can type the function in lower- or uppercase letters.)

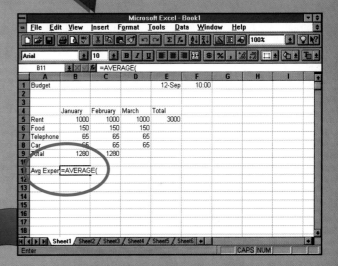

3 Hold down the mouse button and drag the mouse to select cells **B5**, **B6**, **B7**, and **B8**. This step selects the range B5:B8. In the formula bar and in cell B11, you see =AVERAGE(B5:B8. A marquee surrounds the selected range.

Task 30: Calculating an Average

4 Type). Typing) tells Excel that you are finished selecting the range. Excel inserts the range in the parentheses. In the formula bar and in cell B11 you see =AVERAGE(B5:B8).

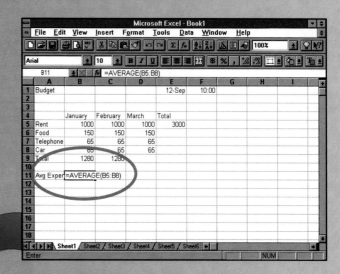

5 Press **Enter**. Pressing Enter confirms the formula. You see the result of the function, 320, in cell B11.

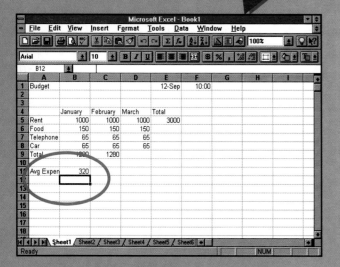

WHY WORRY?

To delete the most recent entry, click the Undo button in the Standard toolbar immediately after entering the AVERAGE function.

Copying a Formula

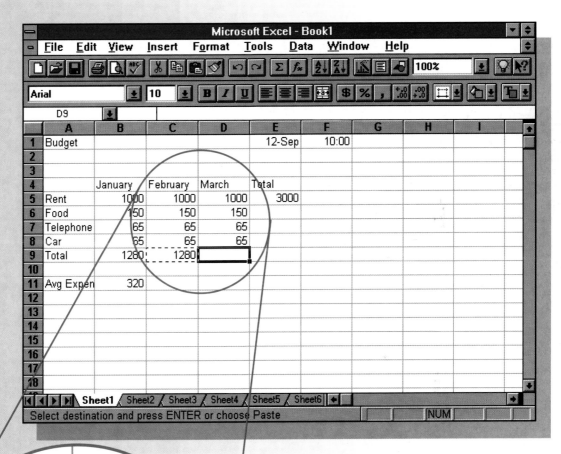

	A	B	C	D	E	F	G	H	I
1	Budget				12-Sep	10:00			
2									
3									
4		January	February	March	Total				
5	Rent	1000	1000	1000	3000				
6	Food	150	150	150					
7	Telephone	65	65	65					
8	Car	65	65	65					
9	Total	1280	1280						
10									
11	Avg Expen	320							

Select destination and press ENTER or choose Paste

"Why would I do this?"

When you build your worksheet, you often use the same data and formulas in more than one cell. With Excel's Copy command, you can create the initial data or formula once, and then place copies of this information in the appropriate cells. You do not have to go to each cell and enter the same data. For example, you might want to copy a formula across a totals row. That way you wouldn't have to type each formula to add up the row of numbers.

109

Task 31: Copying a Formula

1 Click cell **C9**. C9 contains the formula you want to copy.

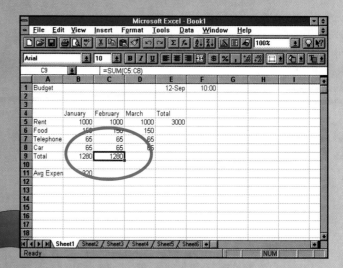

2 Click the **Copy** button on the Standard toolbar. A dashed marquee surrounds the cell you are copying. The message Select destination and press ENTER or choose Paste appears in the status bar to remind you to complete the task.

3 Click cell **D9**. This step selects cell D9. This cell is where you want the copy to appear.

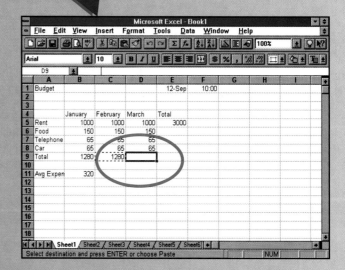

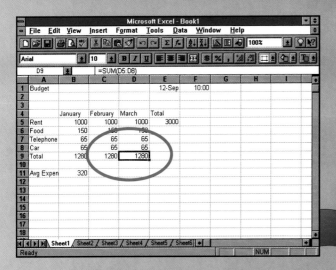

4 Click the **Paste** button on the Standard toolbar. Then press **Esc** to remove the copy marquee. Clicking the Paste button pastes a copy of the data into the cells. The result of the formula appears in cell D9, and the formula bar contains the formula.

NOTE ▼

The copied formula references the current column by *relative addressing*. With relative addressing, Excel automatically adjusts the cell references in the copied formula to reflect the cells at the new location.

5 Click cell **E5** to select the cell that contains the formula you want to copy.

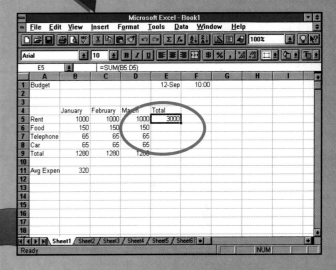

6 Move the mouse pointer to the fill handle in the lower right corner of cell E5 until the mouse pointer changes to a cross. Then drag the fill handle into cells **E6**, **E7**, **E8**, and **E9**. Click cell **E6**. Excel fills the range E6:E9 with the formula from cell E5.

WHY WORRY?

To undo the Copy, click the Undo button on the Standard toolbar.

Naming a Range

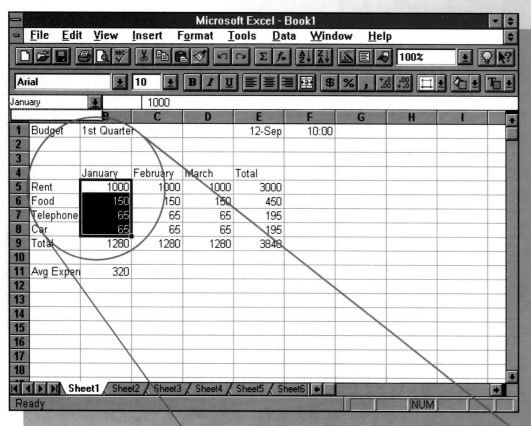

"Why would I do this?"

Naming ranges offers several advantages. Names are easier to remember than cell addresses. You can use range names in formulas. For example, suppose you use the SUM function to add a column of values, and the formula reads =SUM(B5:B8). If you were to give the range B5:B8 the name JANUARY, you could add that column with the function =SUM(JANUARY).

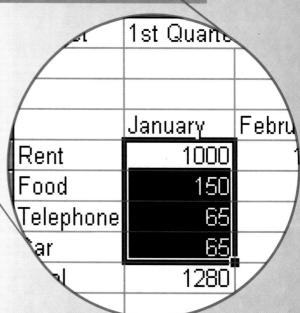

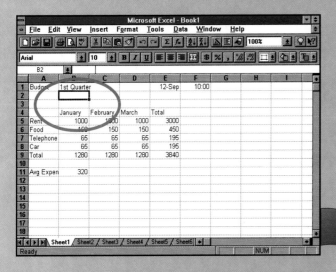

1 Click cell **B1**, type **1st Quarter**, and press **Enter**. This step adds the subtitle to your worksheet. Next, you define a range name for the January values.

2 Select cells **B5**, **B6**, **B7**, and **B8**. This step selects the range you want to name—B5:B8.

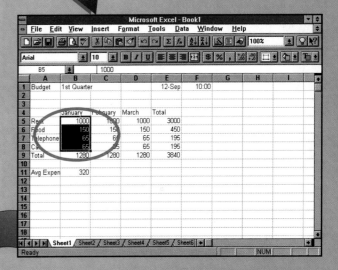

3 Click the down arrow beside the name box in the formula bar. This step highlights the cell address B5 and moves it to the left side of the name box.

Task 32: Naming a Range

4 Type **January**. *January* is the name you want to assign to this range.

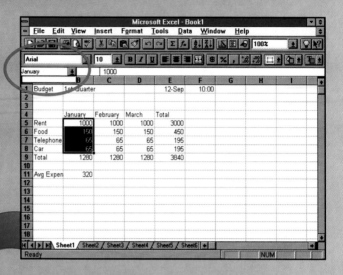

5 Press **Enter**. This step confirms the range you want to name—in this case, cells B5 through B8. Excel adds the range name to the list of names in the name box.

6 Follow steps 2-5 to assign the name *February* to the range C5:C8.

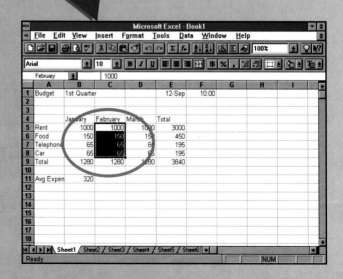

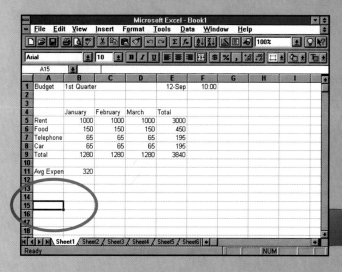

Click cell **A15**. A15 is the first cell in the range in which you want the list of names to appear.

NOTE

The list of names is two columns wide and as many rows long as there are names. Be careful not to place the table of names where it overwrites any data.

Click **Insert** in the menu bar, click **Name**, and then click **Paste**. This step selects the Paste Name command. Excel displays the Paste Name dialog box.

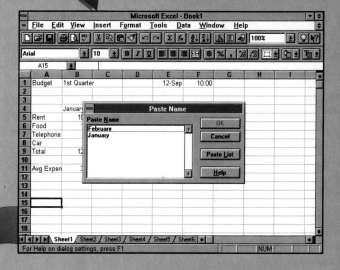

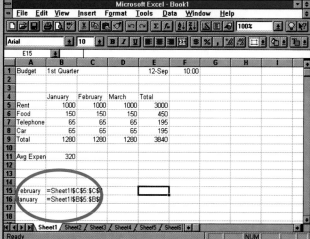

Click the **Paste List** button. Then click any cell to deselect the range. This step inserts the two-column table in a range beginning with cell A15. The first column lists the names in alphabetical order; the second column lists the range coordinates.

WHY WORRY?

To delete a range name, select the Insert Define Name command, highlight the name in the Names in Workbook list box, and click Delete. Then click OK.

115

PART IV

Managing Files

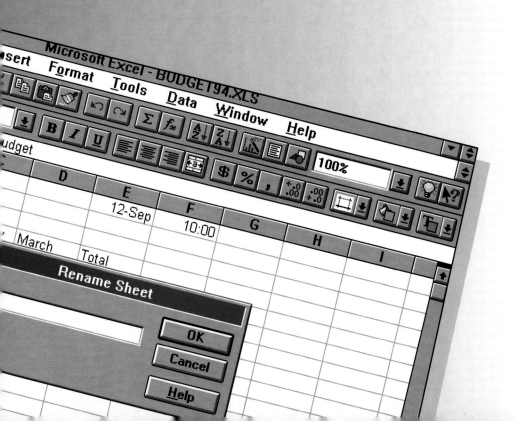

Part IV: Managing Files

This part gives you details about managing workbook files in Excel. You learn how to save your work, abandon a workbook, create a new workbook, open a workbook, find a workbook, close a workbook, and rename the sheets in a workbook. You might already be familiar with using windows inside applications such as Excel. If you want to skip the first part of this section, feel free to do so, but be sure to read the tasks on how to find a workbook and rename sheets within a workbook.

Excel does not automatically save your work, so you should save every five or ten minutes. If you don't save your work, you could lose it. Suppose that you have been working on a worksheet for a few hours and your power goes off unexpectedly—an air conditioning repairman at your office shorts out the power, a thunderstorm hits, or something else causes a power loss. If you haven't saved, you lose all your hard work. Of course, you should also make backup copies on floppy disks from time to time.

Saving a file that you previously saved is slightly different from saving a newly created workbook. When you save a workbook you saved before, you save the current version on-screen and overwrite the original version on disk. This means you always have the most current version of your file stored on disk.

If you want to keep both versions—the on-screen version and the original—you can use the File Save As command to save the on-screen version with a different name. Saving a file with a new name gives you two copies of the same worksheet with differences in their data. When you save a file with a new name, you also can save the file in a different directory or drive.

Saving a workbook does not remove it from the screen. This requires closing the workbook. Whether you've saved a workbook or not, you can close it using the File Close command.

You can open more than one workbook at a time. For example, you might have two separate workbooks that contain related information. While using one workbook, you can view the information in another.

Having both workbooks open and in view makes this possible. The number of workbooks you can open depends on the amount of memory available in your computer.

When you open several workbooks, they can begin to overlap and hide workbooks beneath other workbooks. Excel lets you rearrange the workbooks so that some part of each workbook is visible. Arranging the open windows into smaller windows of similar sizes is one of several arrangement options you can choose from. This is called *tiling windows*. Tiling windows is handy when you want to compare the figures in two workbooks side by side. You can use the Window Arrange Tiles command to arrange the windows in the tiled effect. If you want to display one workbook after you are finished using the tiled window arrangement, close the workbooks you do not want displayed and select the Window Arrange All command. The workbook you want to display fills the screen.

Excel's new Find File command lets you search for a workbook using any search criteria. For example, you can find a workbook using its file name, disk, or directory as search criteria. You can choose the Find File command on the File menu; or when you choose the Open command, you can click the Find File button in the Open dialog box. Either way, Excel can quickly find the file you want to use.

A new Excel workbook has 16 sheets and can contain as many as 255 sheets (depending on your computer's available memory). The sheets are named Sheet1 through Sheet16. You can rename sheets to clearly identify the contents of each sheet. For example, you can rename Sheet1 to QTR 1, Sheet2 to QTR 2, and so on.

In this part, you are introduced to the essential file management skills that you will need in order to work with any files in Excel.

TASK 33

Saving a Workbook

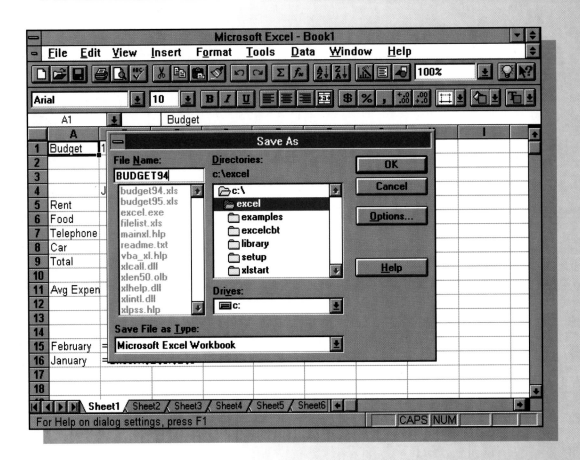

"Why would I do this?"

Until you save the workbook, your data is not stored on disk. You can lose your data if something happens, such as a power loss. When you need the workbook again, you can retrieve it from the disk. Always save your work every five or ten minutes and at the end of a work session. Then close the workbook if you want to clear the screen. Excel also lets you close a previously saved workbook without saving the changes.

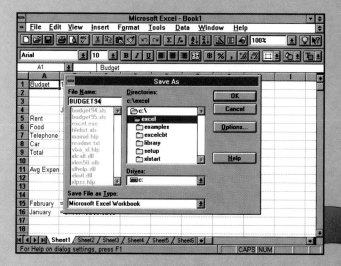

1 Click the **Save** button on the Standard toolbar, which selects the Save command. The first time you save the workbook, Excel displays the Save As dialog box. Type **BUDGET94** in the File Name text box. You can type up to eight characters.

NOTE ▼

The Save As dialog box lists current directories and the current drive. For information on other dialog box options, see your Microsoft Excel documentation.

2 Click **OK**. This step accepts the file name and displays the Summary Info dialog box. You don't have to enter any summary information, but it's a good idea to do so when you create your own workbooks.

NOTE ▼

The Summary Info dialog box summarizes key information about a workbook. You can search for a file based on the information in the summary.

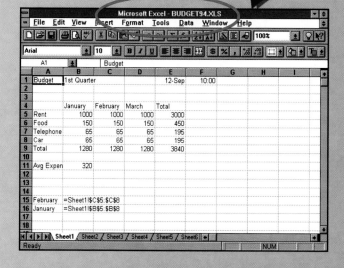

3 Click **OK**. This step returns you to the workbook. The file name, BUDGET94.XLS, appears in the title bar.

WHY WORRY?

If you type a file name that already exists, Excel displays an alert box that asks `Replace existing file?` Click Cancel to return to the Save As dialog box and then type a new name.

TASK 34
Closing a Workbook

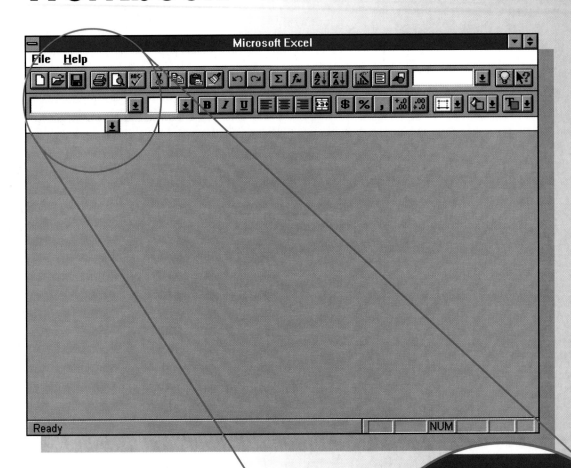

"Why would I do this?"

When you no longer want to work with a workbook, you can use the File Close command to close the workbook. You then can use the Open button on the Standard toolbar to reopen a closed workbook, or use the New Workbook button on the Standard toolbar to create a new workbook, or exit Excel.

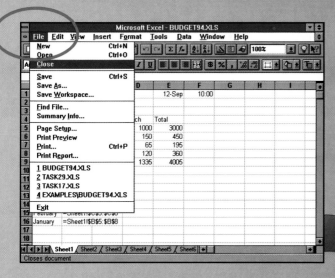

1 Click **File** in the menu bar. This step opens the File menu.

2 Click **Close**. This step selects the File Close command. Excel closes the workbook. You see just two menu options: File and Help. From here, you can open a workbook or create a new workbook.

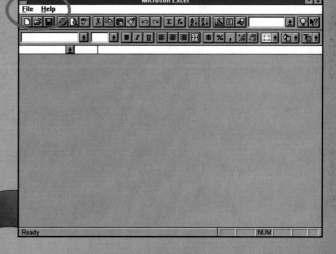

NOTE ▼

You can also use the Control-menu box in the upper left corner of the workbook window on the left end of the menu bar to close the file—simply double-click the Control-menu box.

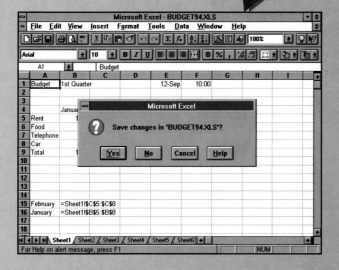

3 If you made changes, Excel displays an alert box that reminds you to save them. Choose Yes to save the changes and close the workbook. If you made changes you don't want to save, choose No to ignore the changes and close the workbook.

WHY WORRY?

If you decide that you do need to make changes, click Cancel in the alert box. Excel takes you back to the workbook, where you can make adjustments.

Creating a New Workbook

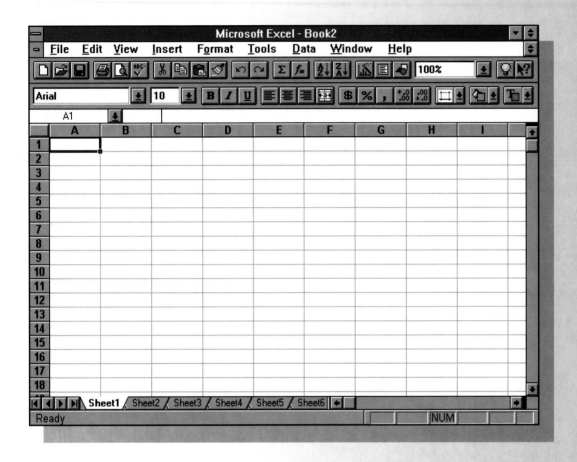

"Why would I do this?"

Excel presents a new, blank workbook when
you first start the program. You can create
another new workbook at any time. Perhaps
you have closed and saved the active workbook
and want to begin a new one.

Create a new workbook and see how it works.
Then you abandon the new workbook.

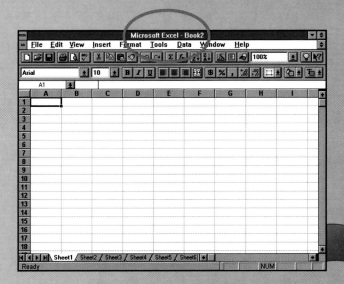

1 Click the **New Workbook** button on the Standard toolbar. Clicking the New Workbook button selects the File New command. A blank workbook appears on-screen. This workbook is titled Book2 (the number varies depending on the number of workbooks you have open).

NOTE ▼

When you start Excel, the program automatically displays a blank work-book. You don't have to use the File New command in this case.

2 Click **File** in the menu bar and then click **Close** to abandon the new workbook. This step selects the File Close command. Excel closes the workbook. As you can see, there are two menu options: File and Help. In the next task, you open a workbook.

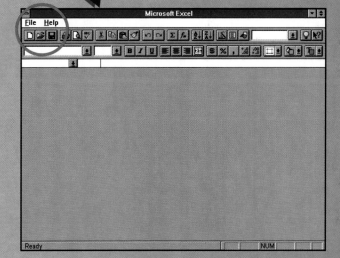

WHY WORRY?

If you don't want to create a new workbook, abandon the workbook.

TASK 36

Opening a Workbook

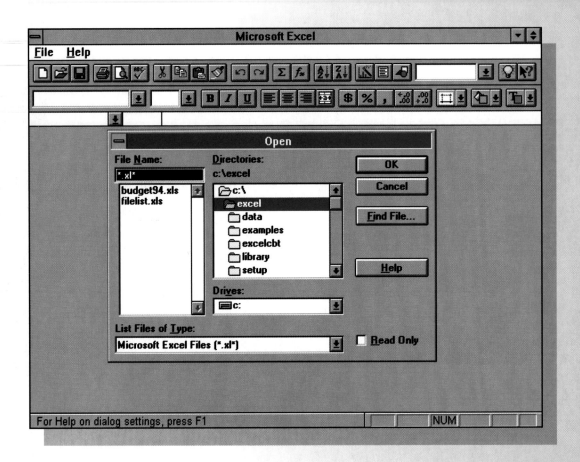

"Why would I do this?"

After you save a workbook, you can view it again or make changes to it later. Or perhaps you want to examine the sample workbooks that came with Excel. The sample workbooks are stored in Excel's EXAMPLES subdirectory.

Suppose you want to work with the BUDGET94 file again. Use the Open button on the Standard toolbar to open the closed workbook file.

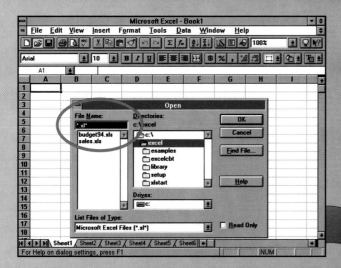

1 Click the **Open** button on the Standard toolbar. Clicking the Open button selects the File Open command. You see the Open dialog box. The insertion point is in the File Name text box.

NOTE ▼

The Open dialog box also contains the Files list and the Directories list. If the file is stored in a different directory, double-click the directory name in the Directories list.

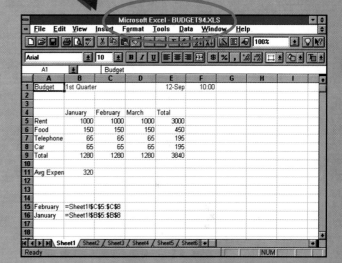

2 If necessary, click the down scroll arrow in the File Name list to find the BUDGET94.XLS file. BUDGET94.XLS is the name of the file you want to open. When you see the file, double-click it. This step selects the file and opens the workbook. Excel displays the workbook on-screen. The file name appears in the title bar.

NOTE ▼

You can type the file name if you know it, or you can use the mouse or the arrow keys to select the file name in the File Name list. You don't have to type the extension.

WHY WORRY?

If you open the wrong workbook, close the workbook and try again.

Finding a Workbook

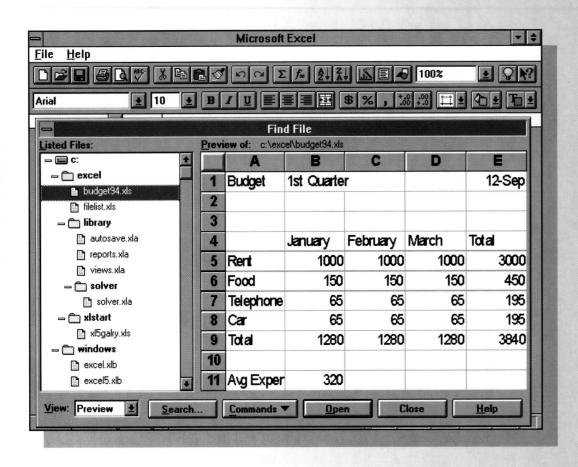

"Why would I do this?"

Excel's new Find File feature enables you to
search for a single file or group of files based on
search criteria you specify. When Excel finds
the files, you can perform a variety of
operations on them such as preview, print,
delete, copy, sort, and much more. The Find
File command is handy when you can't
remember the name of a file. Find the
BUDGET94.XLS with the Find File command.

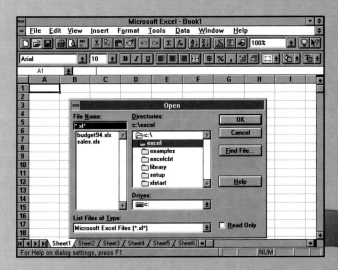

1 Click the **Open** button on the Standard toolbar. This step selects the File Open command. Excel displays the Open dialog box.

2 Click the **Find File** button in the Open dialog box. This step opens the Search dialog box. The insertion point appears in the File Name text box. Notice *.xl* is the current file name and file type. This means that Excel searches for all Microsoft Excel files.

NOTE ▼

You can enter search criteria in the Saved Searches text box and specify advanced search criteria.

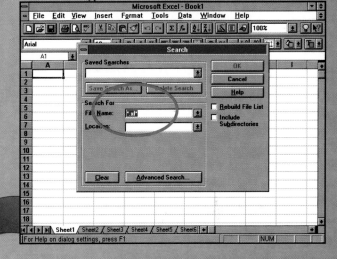

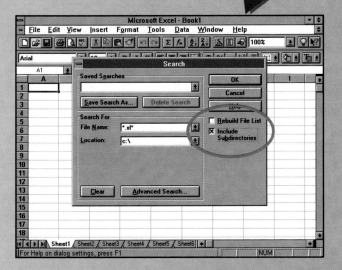

3 Click the down arrow next to the Location text box to see a list of drives. Next, click **C:**. Then click the check box next to **Include Subdirectories**. This step tells Excel which drive you want to search and that you want to search for Microsoft Excel files in all subdirectories.

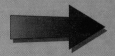

Task 37: Finding a Workbook

4 Click **OK**. This step confirms your choices. Excel displays the Find File window. A list of subdirectories and files appears on the left side of the window. The first file in the list appears in the Preview window.

NOTE ▼

The View options and the Search, Commands, and Open buttons appear at the bottom of the dialog box. For information on other dialog box options, refer to your Microsoft Excel documentation.

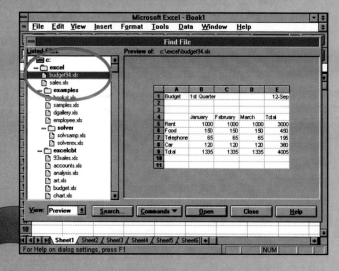

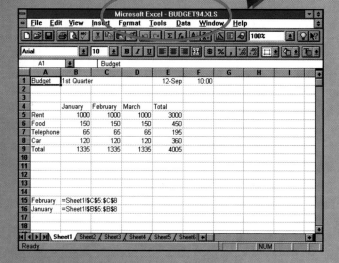

5 Click the **Open** button in the Find File window. This step opens the currently selected file. Excel displays the workbook on-screen. The file name appears in the title bar.

WHY WORRY?

Excel displays the message No matching files found when the program doesn't find any files based on the search criteria you specify. Just click the Search button in the Find File window and try again.

Renaming Sheets

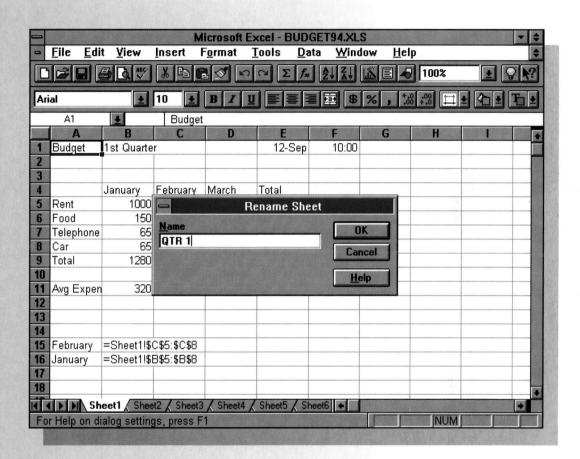

"Why would I do this?"

You can rename sheets in a workbook. This feature lets you change the name of a sheet without altering its contents. Renaming sheets is especially useful if you want to clearly label each sheet in a workbook that contains many worksheets. For example, if you create an annual budget, you can name each sheet tab with January, February, and so on, and then name the final sheet Summary.

Task 38: Renaming Sheets

1 Double-click the **Sheet1** tab. Double-clicking the sheet tab displays the Rename Sheet dialog box. The insertion point is in the Name text box.

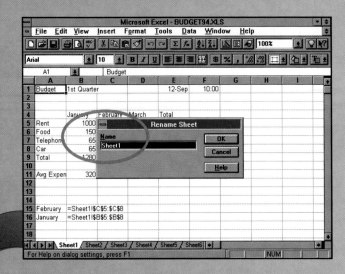

2 Type **QTR 1**. QTR 1 is the new name of the sheet you want to rename. As a rule, you can use a maximum of 31 characters, including spaces.

3 Click **OK**. The new sheet name appears on the first sheet tab. Next, rename the other sheet tabs.

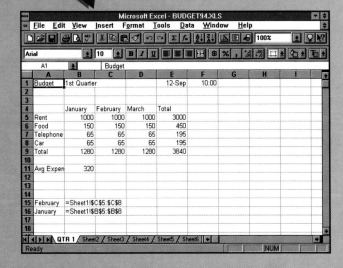

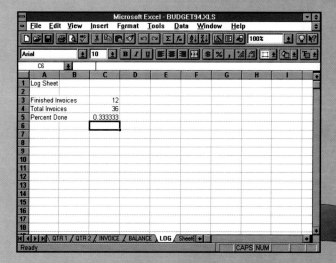

4 Repeat steps 1–3 to rename Sheet2 with the name QTR 2, Sheet3 with the name INVOICE, Sheet4 with the name BALANCE, and Sheet5 with the name LOG.

5 Click the **QTR 1** tab to return to the first worksheet. Then click the **Save** button on the Standard toolbar to save the file.

WHY WORRY?

If you rename the wrong tab, just click the Undo button on the Standard toolbar to undo the renaming operation. Then start over.

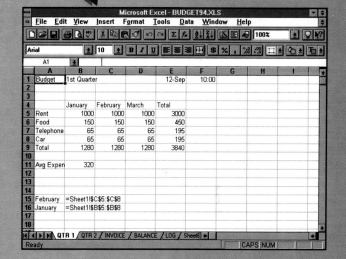

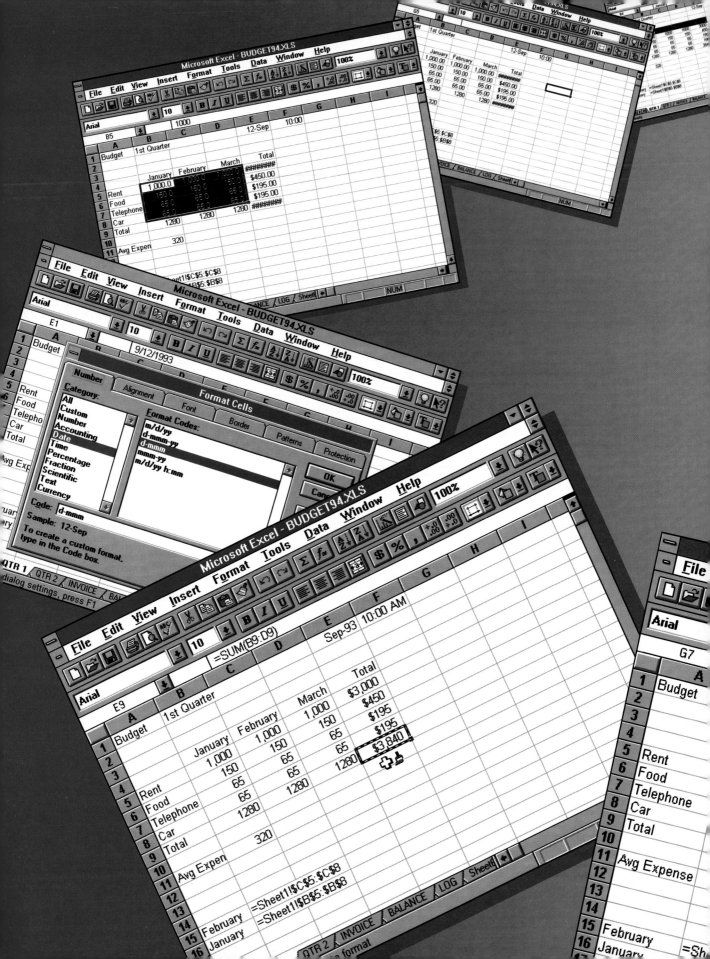

PART V

Formatting the Worksheet

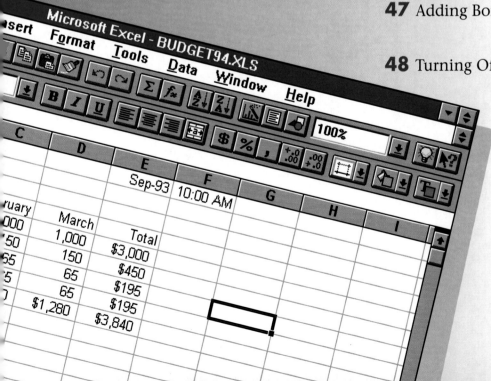

Part V: Formatting the Worksheet

Formatting the worksheet means you can change the appearance of data on your worksheet. With Excel's formatting tools, you can make your worksheet more attractive and readable. In this part you learn how easy it is to center and right-align data in a cell, display dollar signs, commas, and percent signs, change the number of decimal places, and format a date and a time. You also learn how to copy formats with Excel's new Format Painter button, change column width, format individual words, shade cells, add borders, and turn off gridlines.

You can align data in a cell left, center, or right. The default alignment is General. *General alignment* means that numbers are right-aligned and text is left-aligned.

Many times you format cells that don't have numbers in them yet. For example, in your workbook, on the QTR 2 sheet, the cells contain the figures for Rent, Food, Telephone, Car, and Total for the second quarter. You can format those cells with commas even though the cells don't yet contain numbers. When numbers are entered into those cells, they automatically appear with commas.

Determining what format is represented by the symbols in the Number Format dialog box can be confusing at first. You can narrow the list of formats by first selecting a category in the Category list. For example, if you select the Currency category, the first choice is Currency with zero decimal places and negative numbers enclosed in parentheses. The second choice is Currency with zero decimal places; negative numbers are enclosed in parentheses and appear in the color red. The third choice is Currency with two decimal places and negative numbers enclosed in parentheses. The fourth choice is Currency with two decimal places; negative numbers are enclosed in parentheses and appear in the color red.

Excel lets you change the width of any column and the height of any row. You can use the AutoFit feature to quickly change the width of any column. Just double-click the line next to the column letter in the column you want to adjust. Excel automatically changes the width of the column based on the longest entry in that column. If you want to reset the column width to the original setting, choose the Format Column

Width command and click the Use Standard Width check box in the Column Width dialog box.

A *font* is a style of type in a particular typeface and size. Excel displays various fonts and font sizes in the Formatting toolbar. You can use the fonts provided by Excel as well as fonts designed especially for your printer. If Excel does not have a screen version of the printer font you select, it substitutes a font. In this case, the printout looks different than the screen.

You can apply fonts to a single cell or a range of cells. You can also change the font size and font colors. The Font Color button on the Formatting toolbar lets you change font colors in a snap. Varying the font colors to emphasize data makes your worksheet more attractive. Of course, you must have a color monitor and a color printer to benefit from changing font colors.

In Excel, you can apply preset formats to selected data on a worksheet with the AutoFormat command. Generally, you apply one format at a time to a selected range. However, now you can apply a collection of formats supplied by Excel all at once. The formats help you create professional looking financial reports, lists, and large tables.

One of the best ways to enhance the appearance of a worksheet is to add borders to the data on the worksheet. You can use the Borders button on the Formatting toolbar to add boxes around cells and ranges, and you can add emphasis lines anywhere on the worksheet.

Another way to change the overall worksheet display is to remove the gridlines that separate the cells in the worksheet. Your worksheet looks cleaner when you turn off the gridlines.

In this section, you learn some of the most important formatting operations you need for changing the appearance and layout of your worksheets.

Aligning Data

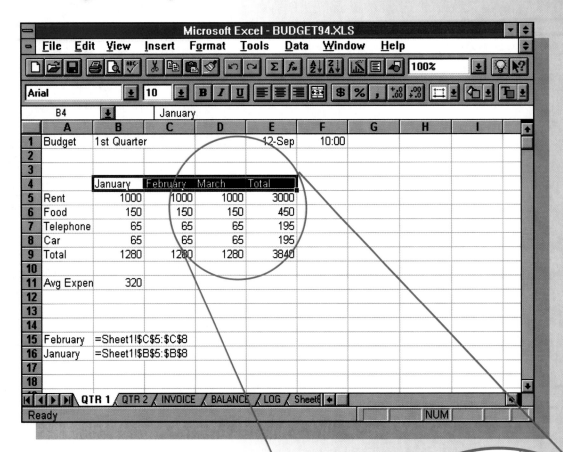

"Why would I do this?"

When you enter data into a cell, numbers, dates, and times automatically align with the right side of the cell. Text aligns with the left side of the cell. You can change the alignment of information at any time. For instance, you might want to fine-tune the appearance of column headings across columns. You can right-align column headings across the columns to line up the headings with the numbers that are right-aligned.

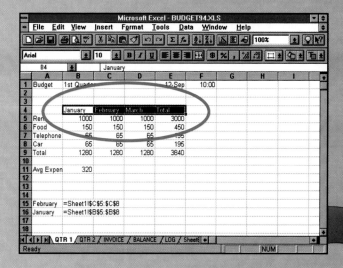

1 Hold down the mouse button and drag the mouse to select cells **B4**, **C4**, **D4**, and **E4**. This step selects the range you want to right-align—B4:E4. Notice that these entries are left-aligned.

2 Click the **Align Right** button on the Formatting toolbar. Then click any cell to deselect the range. This step selects the Right alignment command. Excel right aligns the contents of each cell in the range.

NOTE ▼

Be sure not to align numbers if you want Excel to use the numbers in a formula. If you align numbers left or center, Excel does not recognize the numbers as values and considers the data as text.

WHY WORRY?

To undo the most recent alignment change, click the Undo button on the Standard toolbar.

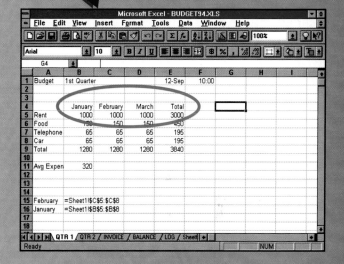

Displaying Dollar Signs, Commas, and Percent Signs

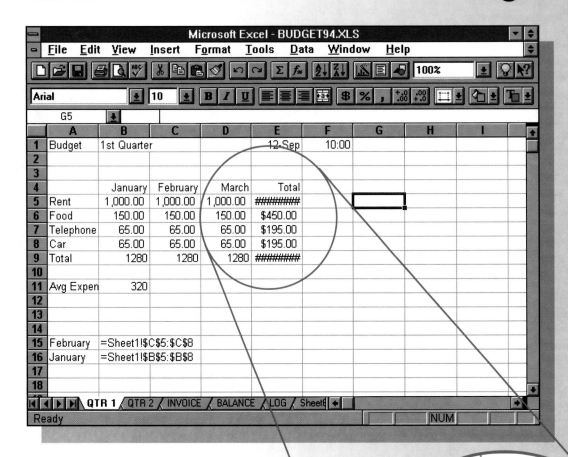

"Why would I do this?"

With Excel's Format Number command, you can display numeric values in many ways. *Formatting* a number means changing the way it is displayed. For instance, you can format the number 600 to look like currency, $600.00. It is important that the numbers in your worksheet appear in the correct format—$600.00 is certainly different than 600%!

Task 40: Displaying Dollar Signs, Commas, and Percent Signs

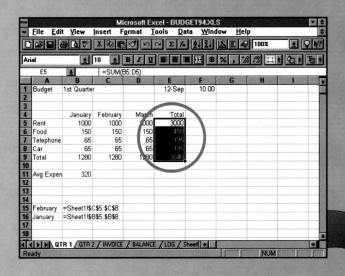

1 Hold down the mouse button and drag the mouse to select cells **E5** to **E9**. This step selects the range E5:E9 in which you want to display dollar signs.

2 Click the **Currency Style** button on the Formatting toolbar. Then click any cell to deselect the range. Clicking the Currency Style button tells Excel to display dollar signs, commas, and two decimal places.

NOTE ▼

If you see number signs (#) in the column, the entry is too long to fit in the column. You must change the column width. You will be learning how to widen a column in a later task in this part.

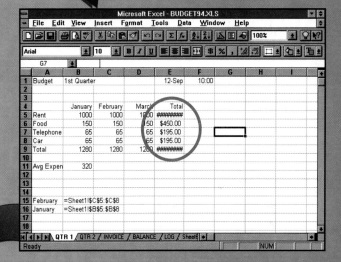

3 Hold down the mouse button and drag the mouse to select cells **B5** to **D8**. This step selects the range B5:D8 in which you want to display commas.

Task 40: Displaying Dollar Signs, Commas, and Percent Signs

4 Click the **Comma Style** button on the Formatting toolbar. Then click any cell to deselect the range. Clicking the Comma Style button tells Excel to display commas and two decimal places.

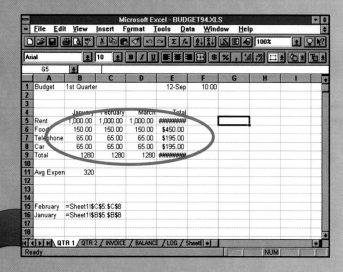

5 Click the **LOG** sheet tab to move to the log worksheet. Then click cell **C5**. This step selects cell C5 in which you want to display a percent sign.

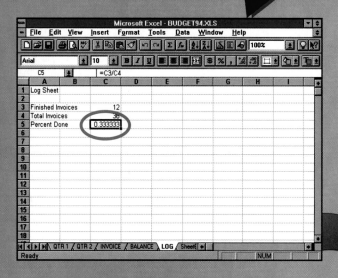

6 Click the **Percent Style** button on the Formatting toolbar. Clicking the Percent Style button tells Excel to display percent signs and zero decimal places.

WHY WORRY?

To undo the most recent formatting change, click the Undo button on the Standard toolbar.

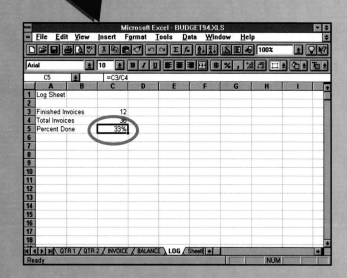

Specifying Decimal Places

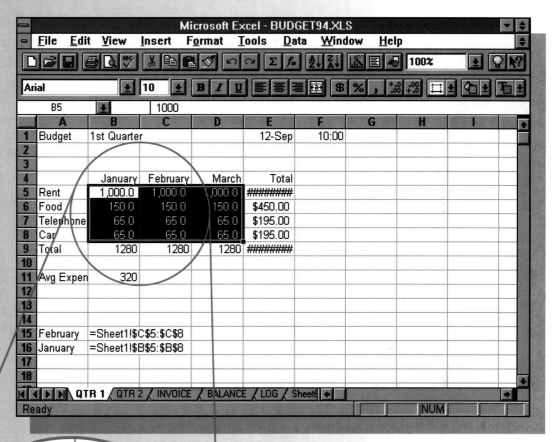

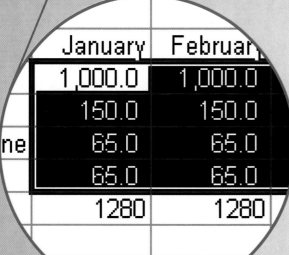

"Why would I do this?"

Decimal places are often added to numbers when you change the format of numbers. For example, Excel assumes you want two decimal places when you change the format to Currency. However, sometimes you don't want any decimal places, or you want a different number of decimal places than are displayed. For example, if your Currency numbers aren't going to have cents, then you don't have to have two decimal places.

Task 41: Specifying Decimal Places

1 Click the **QTR 1** sheet tab to return to the budget worksheet. Then hold down the mouse button and drag the mouse to select cells **B5** to **D8**. This step selects the range B5:D8 in which you want to specify decimal places.

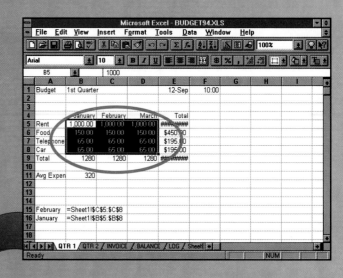

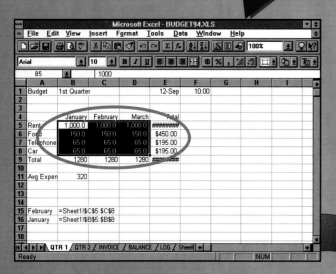

2 Click the **Decrease Decimal** button on the Formatting toolbar. Clicking the Decrease Decimal button moves the decimal point one place to the right. The number of decimal places for the numbers in cells B5 to D8 changed from two to one decimal place. You want zero decimal places for these numbers—so decrease the decimal places again.

3 Click the **Decrease Decimal** button on the Formatting toolbar again. Then click any cell to deselect the range. The number of decimal places for the numbers in cells B5 to D8 changed from one to zero decimal places.

NOTE ▼

If you select zero decimal places, Excel rounds the values to fit this format. If you enter 7.5 in a cell, Excel rounds to 8 when formatting to zero decimal places.

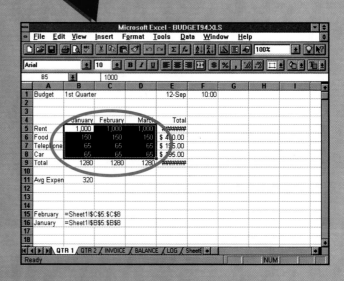

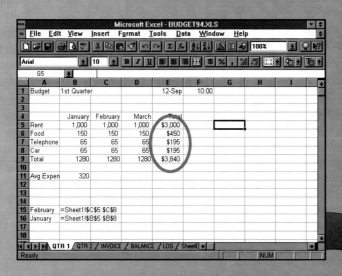

4 Select cells **E5** to **E9**, then repeat steps 2 and 3 to specify zero decimal places for the numbers in the selected range. Be sure to click any cell to deselect the range. The number of decimal places for the numbers in cells E5 to E9 changed from two to zero decimal places.

5 Select cell **B11**. Then click the Currency Style button on the Formatting toolbar. This step selects cell B11 and displays a dollar sign and two decimal places.

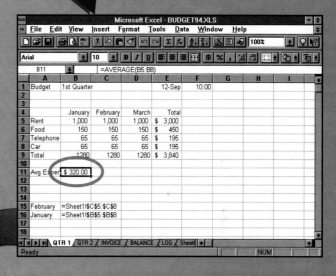

6 Repeat steps 2 and 3 to specify zero decimal places for the number in cell B11. The number of decimal places for the number in cell B11 changed from two to zero decimal places.

WHY WORRY?

To undo the most recent formatting change, click the Undo button on the Standard toolbar.

TASK 42

Changing Date and Time Formats

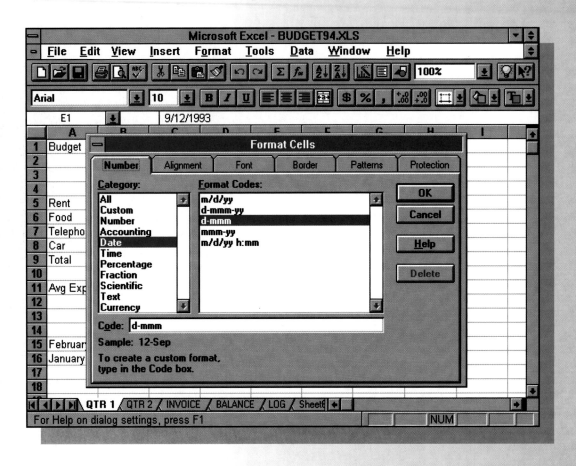

"Why would I do this?"

In Excel, you can enter dates in several different ways so that Excel accepts the date and display in a particular format. If you like, you can change the way Excel displays the date and the time. For instance, 6/1/94 might be clearer to understand as Jun-94. Excel assumes the 24-hour time format unless you enter an a.m. or p.m. designation. The time 10:00 in cell E1 in your budget might be clearer as 10:00 AM.

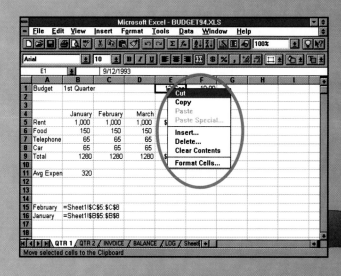

1 Select cell **E1**. Then point to cell **E1** and click the right mouse button. This step selects the cell in which you want to format the date and displays the shortcut menu.

2 Click **Format Cells**. Excel displays Number options in the Format Cells dialog box. The current date format is selected. Because the cell contents is already formatted as a date, only date formats are listed in the dialog box.

NOTE ▼

To display only date formats in the Number Format dialog box, click Date in the Category list.

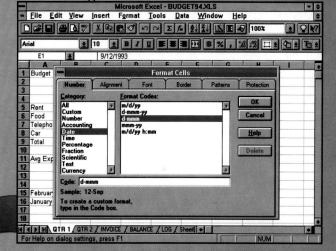

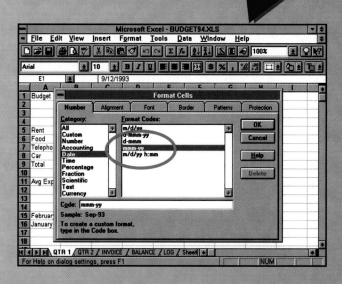

3 Click **mmm-yy**. This format tells Excel to display the date in the format month (mmm) and year (yy). A sample appears at the bottom of the dialog box. The sample uses the value in the selected cell to preview the format.

Task 42: Changing Date and Time Formats

4 Click **OK**. This step confirms the format choice. Excel displays the date in the new format—Sep-93. Next, you change the time format.

> **NOTE** ▼
>
> If you see number signs (#) in the column, the entry is too long to fit in the column. You must change the column width.

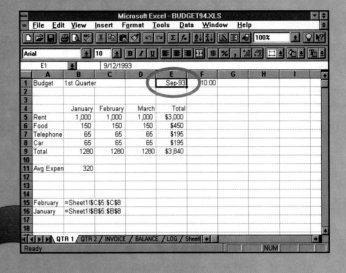

5 Select cell **F1**. This step selects cell F1—the time entry you want to format.

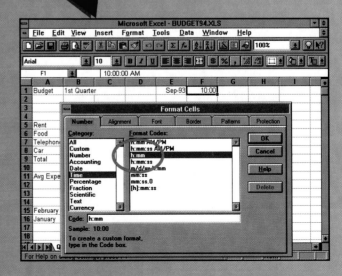

6 Press **Ctrl+1**. Pressing Ctrl+1 selects the Format Cells command. Excel opens the Format Cells dialog box and displays Number options in the dialog box. The current time format is selected. Because the cell contents is already formatted as a time, only time formats are listed in the dialog box.

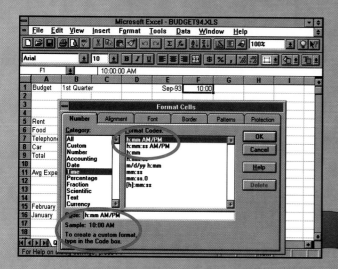

7 Click **h:mm AM/PM**. This format tells Excel to display the time in the format hour (h), minutes (mm), and a.m. or p.m. (AM/PM). A sample appears at the bottom of the dialog box.

NOTE ▼

To display only time formats in the Number Format dialog box, click Time in the Category list.

8 Click **OK**. This step confirms the format choice. Excel displays the time in the new format—10:00 AM.

NOTE ▼

If you see number signs (#) in the column, the entry is too long to fit in the column. You must change the column width.

WHY WORRY?

To undo the most recent formatting change, click the Undo button on the Standard toolbar.

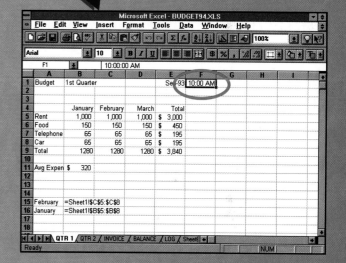

Copying Formats

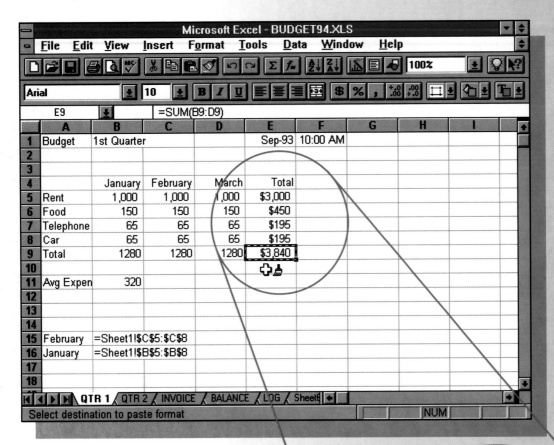

"Why would I do this?"

When the label or the format of a number appears the way you want it, you don't have to repeat the formatting process for the rest of the labels or numbers you want to change. A quick way to copy the formatting of one label or number to all the others that must match it is to use the Format Painter button.

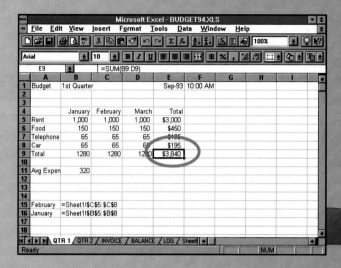

1 Click cell **E9**. This step selects the cell that has the formats you want to copy.

2 Click the **Format Painter** button on the Standard toolbar. Clicking the Format Painter button selects the Copy and Paste Format commands. A copy marquee surrounds cell E9.

NOTE ▼

> The mouse pointer changes to a white cross with a paintbrush. The cross and paintbrush indicate you are copying formats.

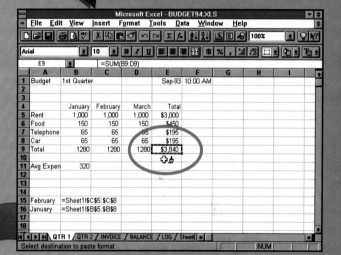

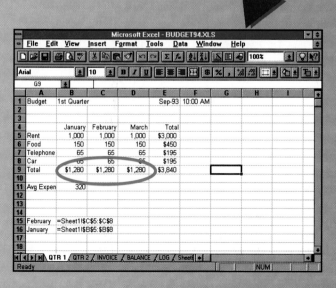

3 Move the mouse to the lower right corner of the active cell and drag the mouse pointer across the cells **B9**, **C9**, and **D9**. Press Esc to remove the copy marquee, and then click any cell to deselect the range.

WHY WORRY?

> To undo the most recent formatting change, click the Undo button on the Standard toolbar.

Changing
Column Width

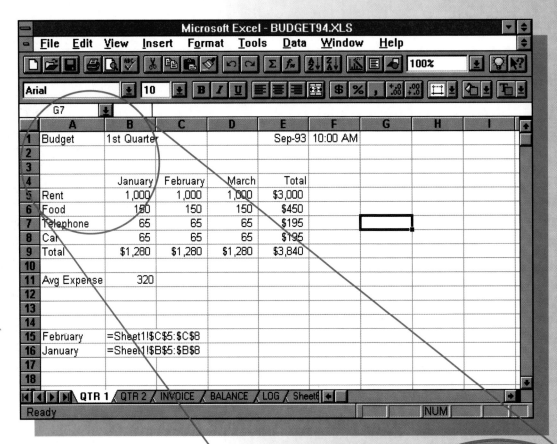

"Why would I do this?"

Number signs (#) in a cell indicate that the column is not wide enough to display the results of the formula. Often, the formatting (and the selected font) makes the entry longer than the default column width. For example, $3,000 is only six characters, but if you format the number as currency with two decimal places, the number appears as $3,000.00. This number requires nine spaces.

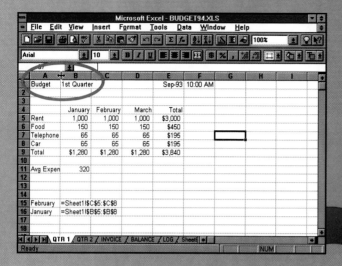

1 Move the mouse pointer to the line to the right of the column letter A of column A. This is the column you want to adjust. The mouse pointer changes to a double arrow.

NOTE ▼

You can also use the AutoFit feature to change column width. You double-click the line to the right of the column you want to adjust. Double-clicking on the line automatically adjusts the width of the column based on the longest entry in the column.

2 Hold down the mouse button. Drag the mouse to make the column the correct width. Excel widens the column.

NOTE ▼

If some entries still spill over into the next column, or if some cells still display number signs, you must widen the column even more.

WHY WORRY?

To undo the most recent formatting change, click the Undo button on the Standard toolbar.

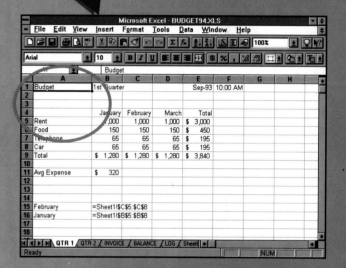

Formatting Cell Contents

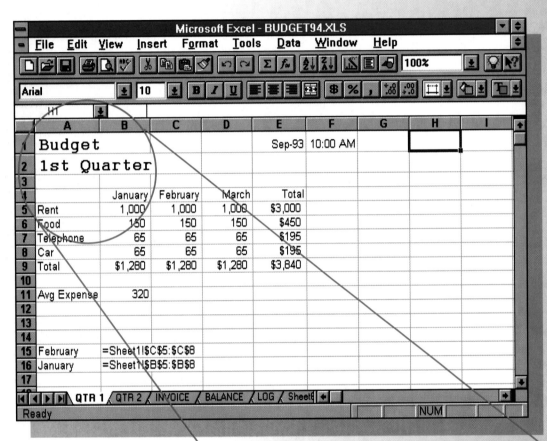

"Why would I do this?"

To bring attention to important words and numbers in a worksheet, you can change the font, font size, font style, and font color. You can change the font for a title to Times New Roman, for example, to enhance the text. You can specify styles such as bold, italic, and underline to emphasize significant words and numbers.

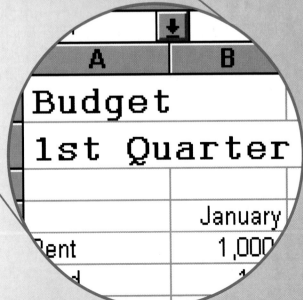

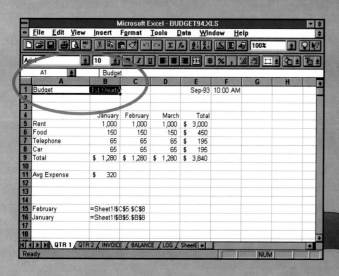

1 Select cells **A1** and **B1**. This step selects the title and subtitle—the text you want to change.

2 Click the down arrow next to the Font box on the Formatting toolbar. This step displays the list of fonts.

NOTE ▼

The fonts in the list can vary, depending on the type of printer you have and the fonts installed.

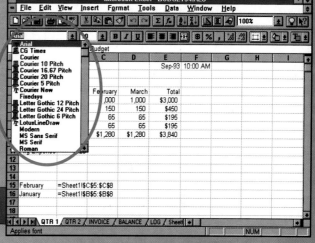

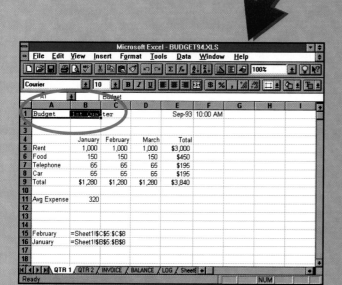

3 Click any font in the list. We chose Courier. This step changes the font for the text in the selected range. The text appears bigger than it was before because it spills over into the adjacent cell. Next, you change the font size to a larger font to emphasize it more.

4 With cells A1 and B1 selected, click the down arrow next to the Font Size box on the Formatting toolbar. This step displays the list of font sizes.

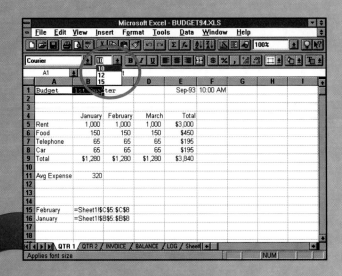

5 Click a larger font size (a higher number). We chose 15. This step changes the font size for the title and subtitle. Next, bring more attention to the titles by applying bold to them.

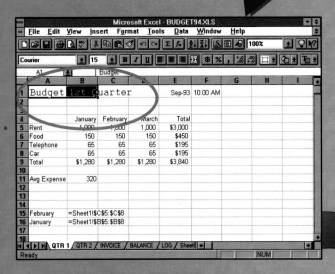

6 Click the **Bold** button on the Formatting toolbar. Then click any cell to deselect the range and see the changes. Clicking the Bold button applies bold to the selected cells—in this case, A1 and B1. 1st Quarter would look better if it appeared below Budget. Move the subtitle to cell A2.

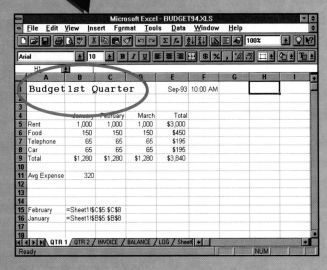

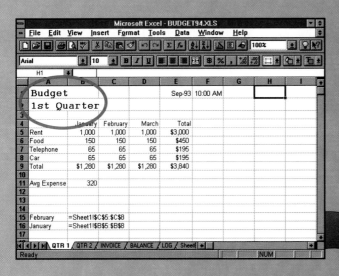

7 Move the subtitle in cell B1 to cell A2. If you need help with this step, see Task 15: Moving a Cell. Next underline the column headings.

8 Select cells **B4:E4**. Then click the **Italics** button on the Formatting toolbar. Then click any cell to deselect the range and see the changes. Clicking the Italics button italicizes the data in the selected cells—in this case, B4:E4. Now, remove the italics style.

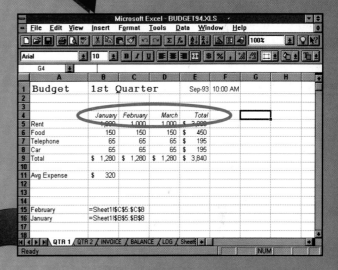

9 Select cells **B4:E4**. Then click the **Italics** button on the Formatting toolbar. Then click any cell to deselect the range and see the changes.

WHY WORRY?

To undo the font change or the font size change, immediately click the Undo button. To undo the bold, italic, and underline font styles, select the formatted cell(s) and then click the Bold, Italic, or Underline button.

Shading Cells

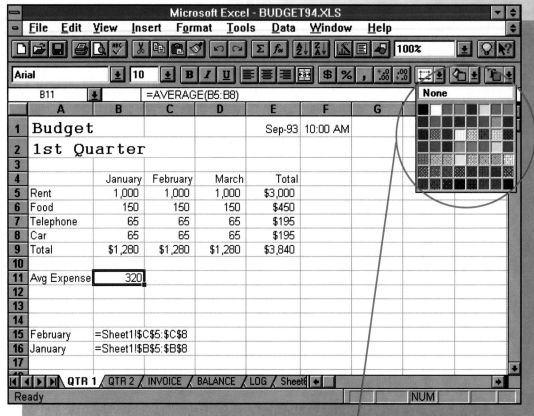

"Why would I do this?"

You can shade cells to draw attention to certain text or numbers in your worksheet. You might want to shade a high or low sales figure, an average, or a grand total.

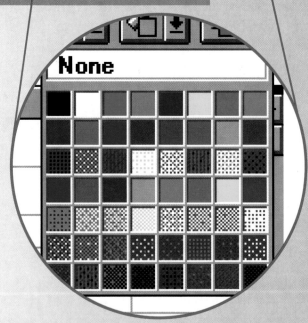

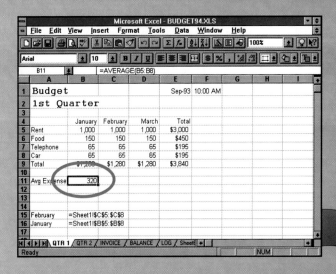

1 Click cell **B11**. This is the cell you want to shade.

2 Click the down arrow next to the **Color** button on the Formatting toolbar. Clicking the Color button displays a color palette below the Color button.

NOTE ▼

Depending on your printer, the shading might print differently than it appears on-screen or not at all.

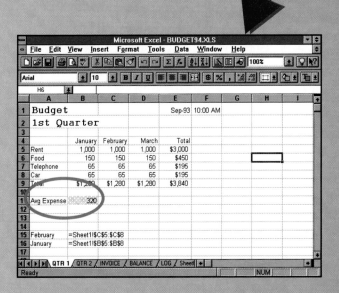

3 In the last column of the palette, click the fifth color from the top. This step selects a light dotted pattern. Then click any cell to deselect the range. On-screen, you see the shading of cell B11 change.

WHY WORRY?

To remove the shading, immediately click the Undo button on the Standard toolbar.

TASK 47

Adding Borders

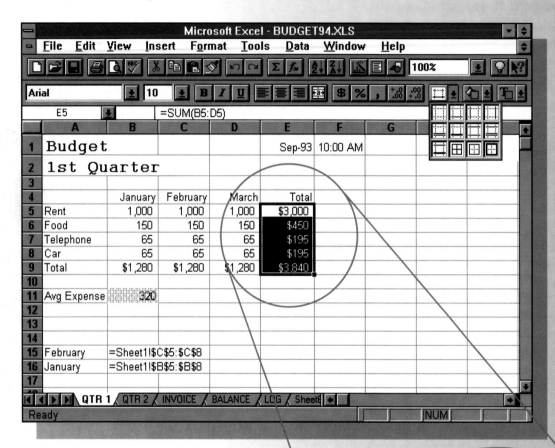

"Why would I do this?"

Excel's Border command lets you add boxes around cells and ranges with either a single or double line. For example, you can have a single thick outline border that creates a box to emphasize the title for the worksheet. Or you can have a double underline on the bottom of cells to bring attention to totals.

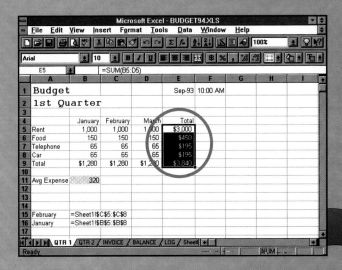

1 Select cells **E5** to **E9**. This step selects the range you want to outline—E5:E9.

2 Click the down arrow next to the Borders button on the Formatting toolbar. Clicking the Borders button displays a palette of border samples below the Border button.

NOTE ▼

The outline still can be hard to see because the gridlines are displayed on-screen.

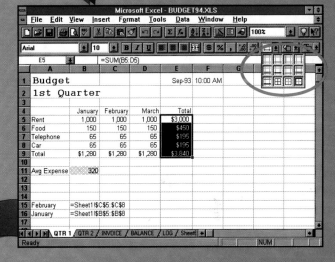

3 In the last column of the palette, click the last border sample. Then click any other cell to deselect the range so you can see the outline better. This step tells Excel to outline the edges of the range with a thick single line.

WHY WORRY?

To remove the outline, immediately click the Undo button on the Standard toolbar.

Turning Off Gridlines

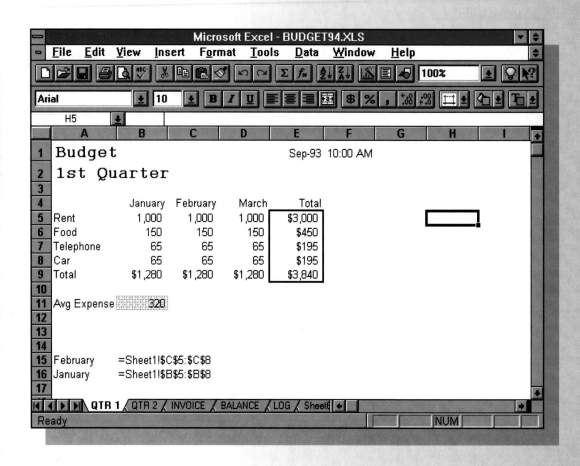

"Why would I do this?"

Another way to make your worksheet look more
attractive is to turn off the gridlines that separate the cells in the worksheet. Your worksheet
seems cleaner on the white background without
the grids. You might want to turn off gridlines
in your worksheets to see how the data looks
when printed on white paper.

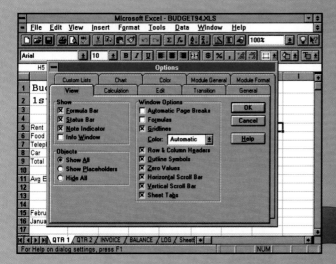

1 Click **Tools** in the menu bar, then click **Options**. Now click the **View** tab. Excel displays the View options in the Options dialog box.

2 Click the check box next to **Gridlines** in the Window Options area. This step deselects the Gridlines option.

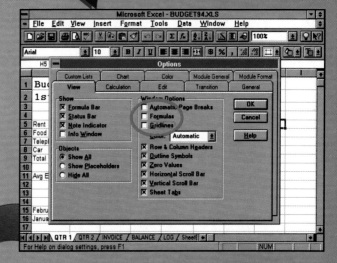

3 Click **OK**. This step confirms your choice. The gridlines no longer appear in the worksheet. Now click the Save button on the Standard toolbar to save the file.

WHY WORRY?

If you change your mind and you want to turn on the gridlines again, immediately click the Undo button in the Standard toolbar. Or you can click the check box next to Gridlines to select the Gridlines option in the Options dialog box.

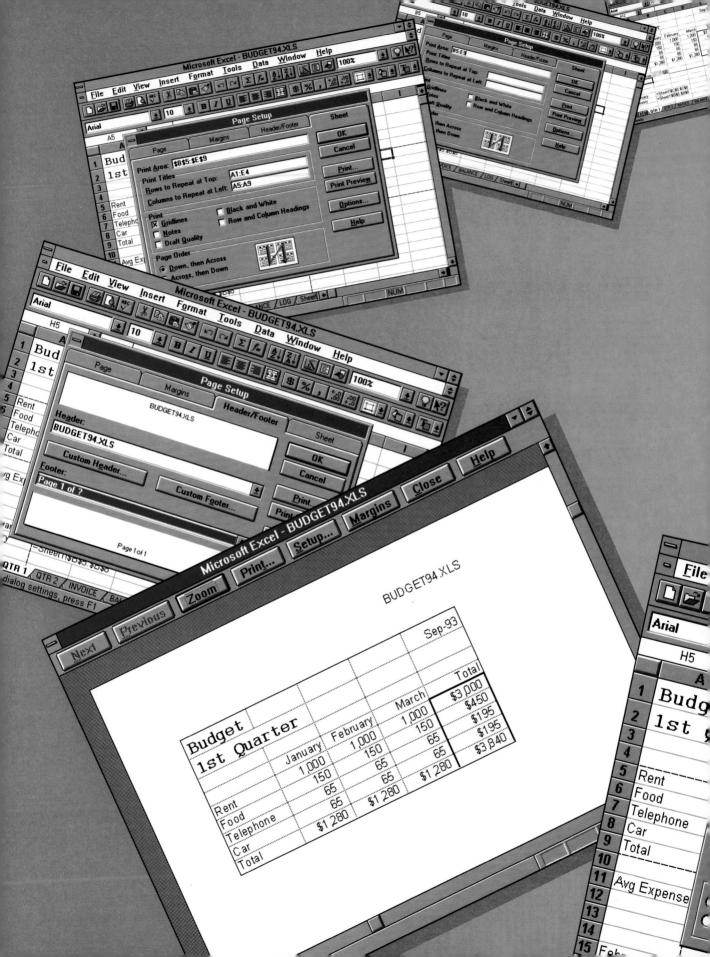

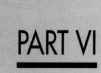

PART VI

Printing the Worksheet

Part VI: Printing the Worksheet

I n Excel, you can print your worksheets using a basic printing procedure or you can enhance the printout using several print options. It is fairly simple to print a worksheet in Excel.

First, you set up the format for your printout. You can insert manual page breaks in your worksheet to split the worksheet on two or more pages. Otherwise, Excel automatically sets the page breaks. There are three ways to set page breaks: 1) at the right side of each page, letting Excel break the pages at the bottom; 2) at the bottom of each page, letting Excel break the pages on the right side; and 3) at the bottom and right side of a page. Page breaks remain on the worksheet until you remove them. Establishing new page breaks does not change existing page breaks. It just adds to them.

You will find most print options in the Page Setup dialog box. In Excel 5, the Page Setup dialog box contains four types of options: Page, Margins, Header/Footer, and Sheet. You can move from one set of options to another by clicking the appropriate tab in the Page Setup dialog box.

There are several important Sheet options you might find useful. You can tell Excel what part of the worksheet you want to print using the Print Area option. For large worksheets, you might want to print column headings at the top with the Repeat Rows at Top option. You can print row headings at the left side of each page with the Repeat Columns at Left option.

With Excel's Print Preview feature, you can review the appearance of the printed worksheet before you produce the final output. The first page of the worksheet appears as a reduced image in the Print Preview screen. However, you can use the Zoom feature in Print Preview to magnify the view. This allows you to inspect the printout more closely. Then, when you click the Zoom button again, Excel reduces the view to a smaller image again. You can also change the margins and page setup and start printing from the Preview window. See your Microsoft Excel documentation for complete information.

The first time you use your printer with Excel, it is a good idea to check the Setup options. Excel can use the options and capabilities that are available with each printer. Often, you will need to provide more details about your printer so that Excel knows the capabilities available. If you want to specify details about your printer, choose the File Printer Setup command. Then, you can confirm that you installed the right printer and connected it correctly, or you can switch to a different printer.

The Page and Margins options in the Page Setup dialog box control print enhancements such as orientation, margins, and the size of the printout. The default print orientation is Portrait, which means that the worksheet prints vertically on the paper. You can choose Landscape to print the worksheet sideways or horizontally on the paper. If the worksheet is too wide, you can try decreasing the widths of some cells if possible.

If the worksheet is still too large to print on one page, you can change the top, bottom, left, and right margins. You also might consider reducing the printout using the Adjust To option in the Page Setup dialog box. Some printers will let you reduce or enlarge the printout as it prints. Although 100% is normal size, you can enter the desired reduction or enlargement percentage you want.

The Fit To option prints the worksheet at full size to fit the size of the page. You can enter the number of pages in the Page(s) Wide By and the Tall text boxes to specify the document's width and height. This is useful for printing graphics and charts. This option may not be available on all printers. It is a good idea to experiment with all the print options until you get the results you want.

Excel lets you add headers and footers to print information at the top and bottom of every page of the printout. You can choose the headers and footers suggested by Excel, or you can include any text plus special commands to control the appearance of the header or footer.

It is a good idea to save your worksheets before printing—just in case a printer error or other problem occurs. You won't lose any work since the last time you saved the worksheet. You learn how to print your worksheet from the Page Setup dialog box. But if you already set up your print options and you're back to the worksheet, you can just click the Print button on the Standard toolbar to print your worksheet.

Now in Excel, the Print dialog box lets you print some or all the sheets within a workbook, a range of pages, and multiple copies of the printout.

This part introduces you to the basics of printing the worksheet. With some experimentation and practice, you will be able to create some very interesting print results.

Inserting and Removing Page Breaks

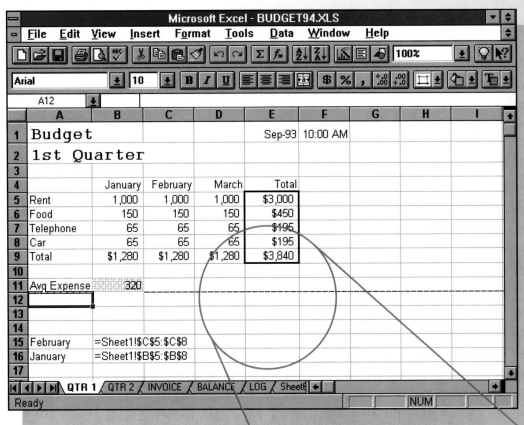

"Why would I do this?"

In Excel, you can control where each new page begins. You can set a manual page break anywhere on the worksheet.

Setting manual page breaks overrides automatic page breaks entered by Excel. With automatic page breaks, Excel decides where page breaks will appear in the worksheet based on standard 8-1/2-by-11-inch paper.

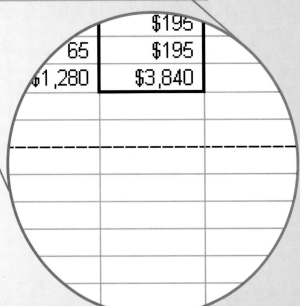

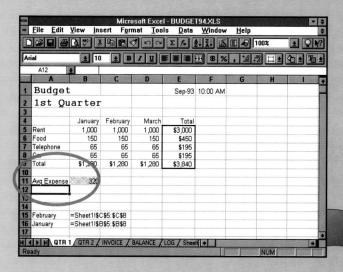

1 Click **A12**. A12 is the cell below where you want to insert a page break. Excel will print everything above row 12 on one page and everything below row 12 on the next page.

NOTE ▼

If you click a cell that is not in the far left column of the worksheet and then select the Options Set Page Break command, Excel inserts manual page breaks above and to the left of the selected cell.

2 Click **Insert** in the menu bar. Then click **Page Break**. The manual page break appears above the active cell.

NOTE ▼

On-screen, manual page breaks have longer, thicker dashed lines than automatic page breaks. These page breaks may be hard to see when gridlines also appear on-screen.

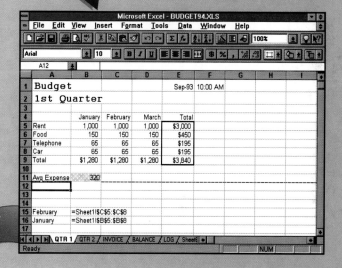

3 Click **Insert** in the menu bar. Then click **Remove Page Break**. The manual page break disappears above the active cell.

WHY WORRY?

If you insert the page break in the wrong place, just select the cell immediately below and to the right of the page break line(s). Then, delete the page break with the Insert Remove Page Break command.

TASK 50

Selecting a Print Area

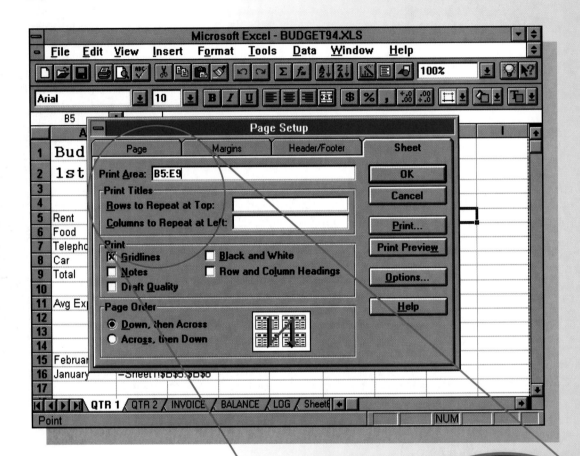

"Why would I do this?"

Often, you will want to print specific portions of a worksheet, such as a range of cells. You can single out an area as a separate page and then print that page. Excel will print only the established print area. If the area is too large to fit onto one page, Excel will break it into multiple pages.

Let's select a print area that includes the range B5:E9.

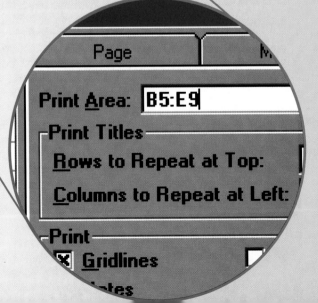

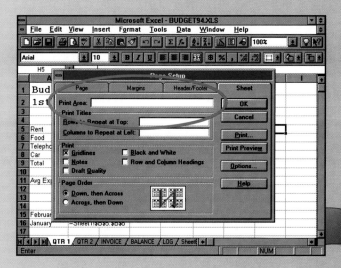

1 Click **File** in the menu bar. Then click **Page Setup**. Excel displays the Page options in the Page Setup dialog box. Click the **Sheet** tab to display the Sheet options. Notice the Print Area text box at the top of the dialog box.

2 Click in the **Print Area** text box to display the insertion point. Then type **B5:E9**. This step specifies the range B5:E9—the range where you want to select a print area.

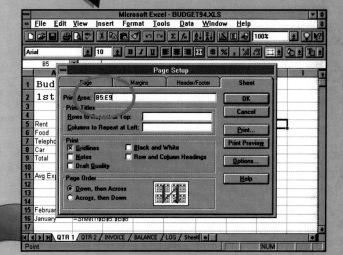

NOTE ▼

Do not include the title, subtitle, and column and row headings in the print area. If you do, Excel will print the labels twice. In the next task, we will use these labels to print the column and row headings on every page.

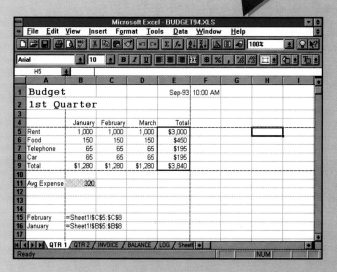

3 Click **OK**. This step confirms your choice. The automatic page breaks appear to the right and on the bottom of the range B5:E9.

WHY WORRY?

To remove the print area, delete the cell coordinates in the Print Area text box. Excel does not have an Undo command to remove the print area.

Printing Column and Row Headings

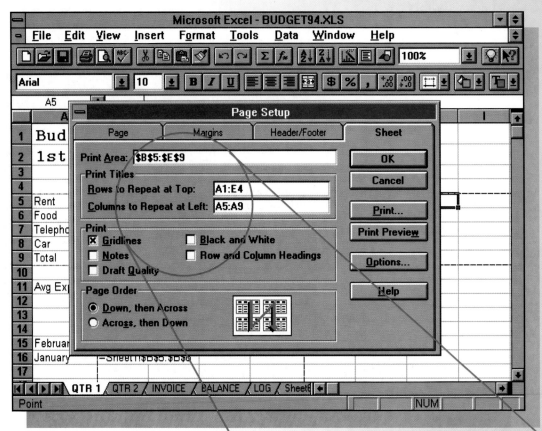

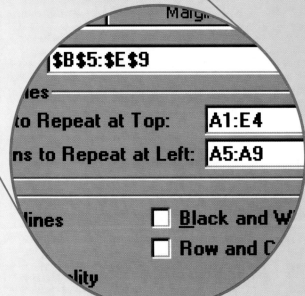

"Why would I do this?"

Excel provides a way for you to select labels and titles that are located on the top edge and left side of your worksheet, and print them on every page of the printout. This option is useful when a worksheet is too wide to print on a single page. The extra columns will be printed on subsequent pages without any descriptive information unless you use the Repeat Rows at Top and Repeat Columns at Left options.

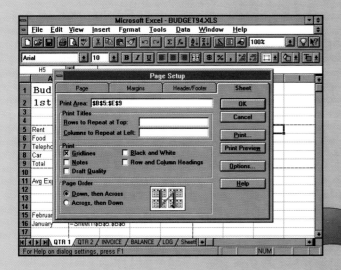

1 Click **File** in the menu bar. Then, click **Page Setup**. This step selects the File Page Setup command. Excel displays the Sheet options in the Page Setup dialog box, the last set of options we worked with.

2 Click in the **Rows to Repeat at Top** text box. The insertion point appears in the box. Then type **A1:E4**. This step specifies the range A1:E4—the range you want to repeat at the top of every page.

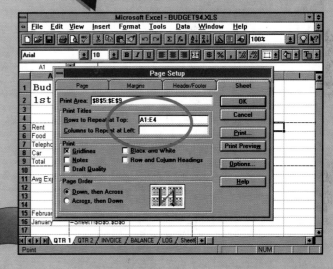

3 Click in the **Columns to Repeat at Left** text box. The insertion point appears in the box. Then type **A5:A9**. This step specifies the range you want to repeat at the left side of every page. Click **OK**.

WHY WORRY?

To remove the rows and columns you want to repeat, delete the cell coordinates in the Rows to Repeat at Top and Columns to Repeat at Left text boxes.

TASK 52

Adding Headers and Footers

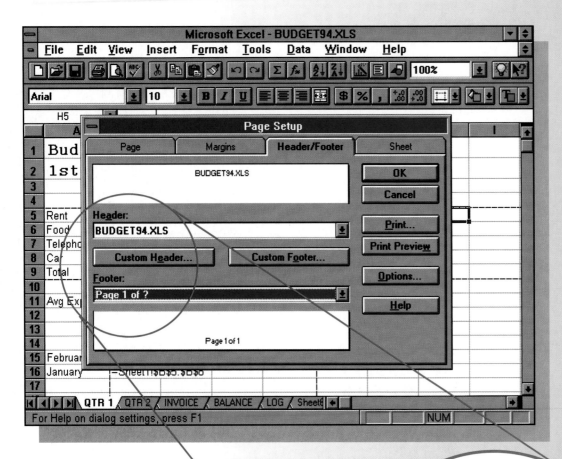

"Why would I do this?"

Headers and footers are lines of text that you can print at the top and bottom of every page in a print job—headers at the top, footers at the bottom. You can include any text, the current date and time, the file name, and even format the information in a header and footer.

Let's create a header that contains the file name and a footer that will number the pages in our budget worksheet.

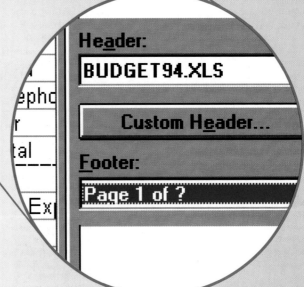

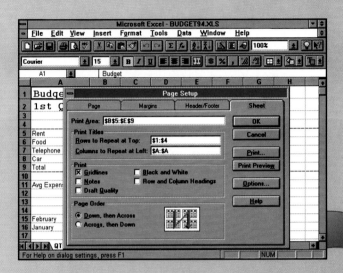

1 Click **File** in the menu bar. Then click **Page Setup**. This step selects the File Page Setup command. Excel opens the Page Setup dialog box.

2 Click the **Header/Footer** tab to display the Header/Footer options. Notice the header and footer options in the box. Excel uses the name of the sheet, QTR 1, as the header.

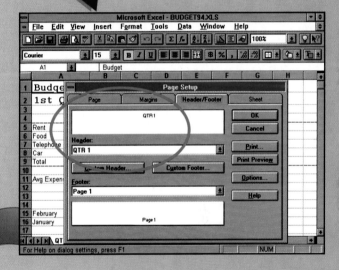

3 Click the down arrow next to the **Header** text box. A list of suggested header information displays. Scroll through the list until you see BUDGET94.XLS. Then click it. The sample header appears at the top of the box. Notice that BUDGET94.XLS is centered. Also notice that the footer Page 1 appears in the footer sample.

Task 52: Adding Headers and Footers

4 Click the down arrow next to the **Footer** text box. A list of suggested footer information displays. Scroll through the list until you see Page 1 of ?. Then click it. The sample footer appears at the bottom of the box. Notice Page 1 of 1 is centered.

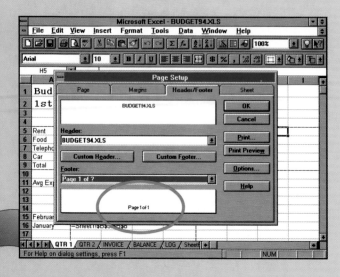

5 Click **OK**. This step closes the Page Setup dialog box. On-screen, you cannot see the header and footer. To do so, you must preview the worksheet.

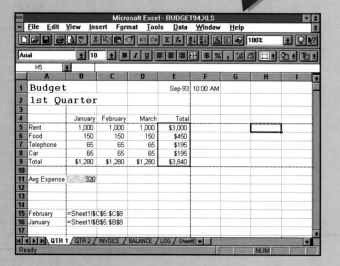

NOTE ▼

You can include special codes in the header or footer. Excel also provides several header and footer options. Refer to your Microsoft Excel documentation for a complete list of codes and formatting options.

WHY WORRY?

If something unexpected prints at the top or bottom of your worksheet, check the Header or Footer text box. If you don't want a header or footer, choose None in the Header or Footer suggestions list.

Previewing the Print Job

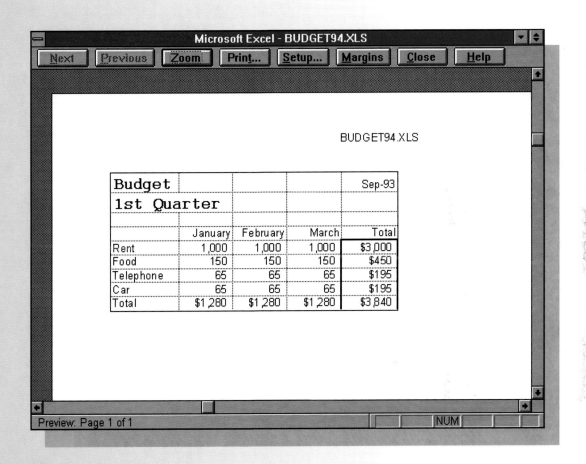

"Why would I do this?"

The Print Preview command lets you see worksheet pages on-screen as they will appear printed on paper, including page numbers, headers, footers, fonts, fonts sizes and styles, orientation, and margins. Previewing your worksheet is a great way to catch formatting errors, such as incorrect margins, overlapped data, boldfaced data, and other text enhancements. You will save costly printer paper and time by first previewing your worksheet.

Task 53: Previewing the Print Job

1 Click the **Print Preview** button on the Standard toolbar (the button with the piece of paper and a magnifying glass). Clicking the Print Preview button selects the Print Preview command. You see a preview of how your worksheet will look when you print it.

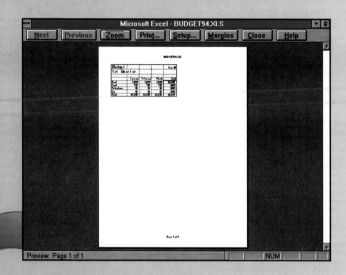

2 Click the **Zoom** button at the top of the screen. This step enlarges the preview to its actual size. This enables you to examine the printout more closely.

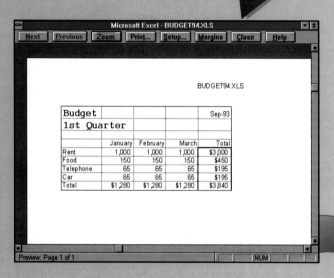

NOTE ▼

To preview the worksheet, your monitor must have graphics capability. Try this procedure. If you see an error message, your monitor probably cannot display the worksheet. You must print the worksheet to see how it looks.

3 To exit the Preview, click the **Close** button. This step returns you to the worksheet.

NOTE ▼

You also can press the Esc key to quit the preview.

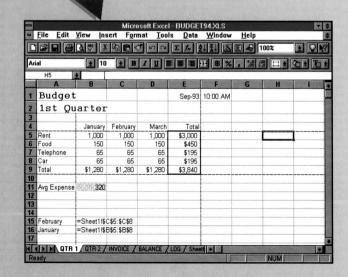

Printing the Worksheet

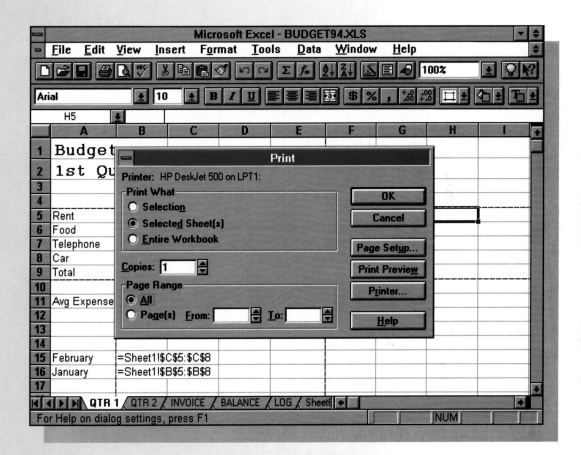

"Why would I do this?"

Excel gives you many print options for customizing the way you print your worksheets. You can change the orientation, margins, or reduce or enlarge the printout to fit on an 8 1/2" x 11" sheet of paper. Refer to your Microsoft Excel documentation for complete information on the options in the Page Setup dialog box.

Let's print the budget worksheet.

Task 54: Printing the Worksheet

1 Click **File** in the menu bar. Then click **Page Setup**. This step selects the File Page Setup command. Click the **Page** tab to display the Page options.

NOTE ▼

Notice the Orientation options at the top of the box. Excel's default orientation setting is Portrait (paper is vertical). Landscape (paper is horizontal) is the orientation we want.

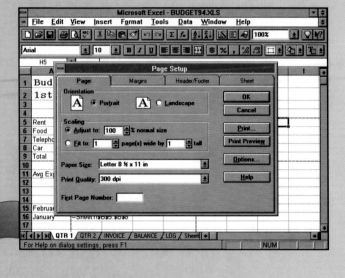

2 Click the **Landscape** option button. This step selects the Landscape orientation. This option tells Excel to print the worksheet sideways.

3 Click the **Margins** tab to display the Margins options. Excel uses the following default margin settings: Left .75", Right .75", Top 1", and Bottom 1". Double-click in the **Top** text box and type **2**. This step sets the new top margin to two inches.

NOTE ▼

You can see the new top margin in the Preview sample in the middle of the box.

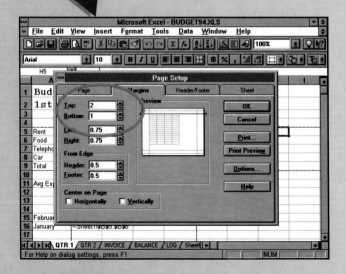

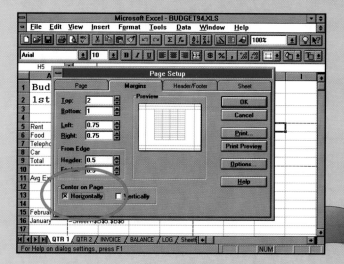

4 Click the **Center on Page Horizontally** check box. Excel will center the page from left to right based on the current left and right margin settings. Now let's print the worksheet.

> **NOTE** ▼
>
> You can see that the worksheet is centered horizontally in the Preview sample in the middle of the box.

5 Click the **Print** button. This step selects the Print command. Excel displays the Print dialog box. You see the name of your printer at the top of the dialog box. Click **OK** to start the print job.

> **NOTE** ▼
>
> When you installed the Excel program, you also installed the printer. If no printer is installed, refer to the Excel manual.

> **WHY WORRY?**
>
> To reset any options in the Page Setup dialog box, follow the same procedure. You cannot use an Undo command to reverse the settings. During a print job, Excel displays a dialog box on-screen. To stop the print job, click Cancel.

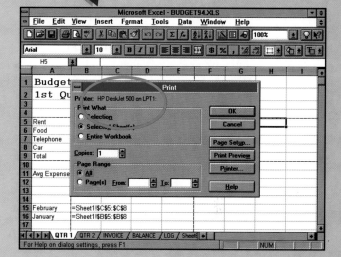

PART VII

Working with Charts

After you create your worksheets, you'll probably want to use the information in a presentation. You can print the worksheet if you only need numerical detail, or you can transform the data in the worksheet into a chart. Charts are great for visually representing relationships between numerical values while at the same time greatly enhancing a presentation.

In Excel, you can create a chart on its own sheet or directly on the worksheet as an embedded chart. You can print and enhance a chart on its own sheet the same way you would an embedded chart. You create the chart on a separate sheet within a workbook, called a *chart sheet*. A chart sheet can save space in a workbook because it is stored on a separate sheet.

An *embedded chart* is a graphic object that displays on the worksheet, along with your worksheet data. This type of chart is easier to use because it is part of the worksheet. You can print any worksheet that contains data, graphics, and an embedded chart. You can save the chart on its own sheet, and an embedded chart with the File Save command as you would any file.

Excel displays the Chart toolbar when you select an embedded chart in a worksheet. You can use the Chart toolbar buttons to change the chart type and add gridlines and a legend. You can also use the Text Box button on the Standard toolbar to add text labels to your charts.

Before you create a chart, you should familiarize yourself with the elements of a chart. The *data series* can be bars, pie slices, lines, or other elements that represent plotted values in a chart. For example, a chart might show a set of bars that have the same pattern. These bars reflect a series of values for the same item—for example, monthly sales figures.

Categories show the number of elements in a data series. You might use two data series to compare the sales of two different offices, and four categories to compare these sales over four quarters. Categories usually correspond to the number of columns that you have selected in your worksheet. *Category labels* describe the categories below the axis. These labels come from the column headings.

The *chart text* includes all the labels on the chart. Most chart text has to be added to the basic chart. You can also format labels by changing the fonts, font sizes, font styles, and colors. Text is useful for explaining various elements on the chart. The *value axis* is the vertical axis, sometimes referred to as the *Y axis*. It represents the values of the bars, lines, or plot points. Excel automatically assigns values to this axis when you create a chart, but you can override the default settings and set the minimum and maximum values. You can also add a text label to the value axis to describe what the values represent. The *category axis* is the horizontal axis, sometimes referred to as the *X axis*. This axis contains the data series and categories in the chart. If your chart contains more than one category, Excel displays labels that identify each category.

The *plot area* consists of the actual bars, lines, or other elements that represent the data series. Everything outside the plot area helps explain what is inside the plot area. You can format the plot area by changing the patterns and colors of the data series. A *legend* contains the series labels in the chart data. The legend will appear at the right of the chart data. However, you can move the legend anywhere you want on the chart. Excel matches the labels with the *series markers* and provides a "key" to the chart. Excel already knows which chart labels make up the legend. These labels are the data series labels in the first column of the chart range. *Gridlines* are dotted lines you can add to a chart so that you can read the plotted data more easily. You can create three types of gridlines: horizontal, vertical, and a combination of both. After you add the gridlines, you can change their colors and patterns.

Tick marks are small lines that intersect the axis. These marks look like the lines on a ruler. *Tick mark labels* define the categories, values, or series in the chart. For example, the numbers on the vertical axis scale are tick mark labels. You can change the appearance of the tick marks and tick mark labels on the axis line.

You will learn how to create a chart quickly and easily with the ChartWizard. Any Excel feature that ends with the name *Wizard* is designed to lead you step-by-step through an otherwise complex procedure. The ChartWizard guides you through the process of creating an embedded chart. There are several advantages to using the ChartWizard to create an embedded chart: you get help every step of the way; you can preview the sample chart before you finish creating the chart; and you can make changes to the chart as you're creating it at any time you want.

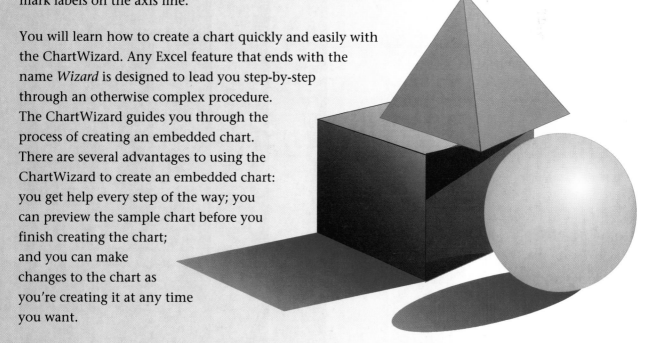

Creating a Chart

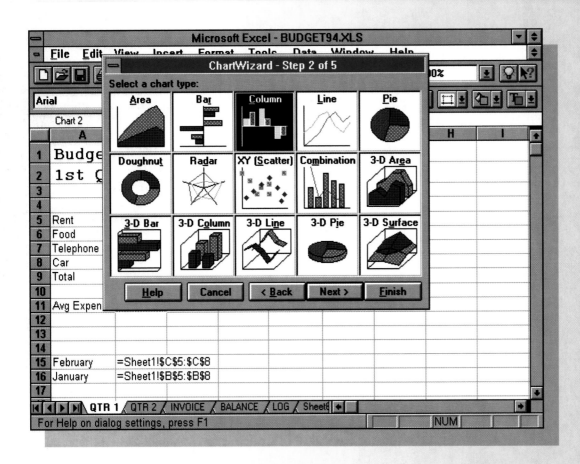

"Why would I do this?"

The easiest way to create a chart in Excel is to
use the ChartWizard feature. The ChartWizard
leads you step-by-step through the tasks for
creating an embedded chart. Excel plots the
data and creates the embedded chart where you
specify on the worksheet. If you are a novice at
creating charts in Excel, you will find that
transforming the worksheet data into a chart
with the ChartWizard is a breeze.

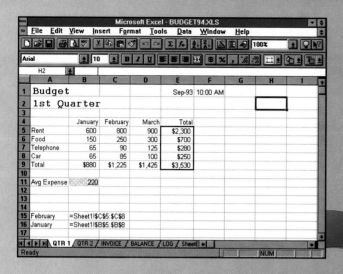

1 Choose **File Page Setup**, click the **Sheet** tab, and remove the coordinates in the **Print Area** text box. Then click **OK**. Notice that the page breaks disappear from the worksheet. Now change the data in the budget according to the figure so that your computer screen matches the screen in this book.

2 Select cells **A4** to **D8**. This step selects the range A4:D8—the range you want to chart.

> **NOTE** ▼
>
> Remember, you must first select data before you can create a chart.

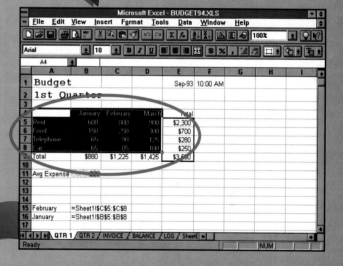

3 Click the **ChartWizard** button on the Standard toolbar. A marquee surrounds the selected data. The mouse pointer changes to a cross-hair pointer. Next to the pointer is a tiny column chart. The ChartWizard cross-hair pointer lets you create a box to specify the size and shape of the chart on the worksheet.

4 Click cell **G1** and drag the cross-hair pointer to cell **M12**. Then release the mouse button. Cell G1 is where you want the upper left corner of the chart to appear. Cell M12 is where you want the lower right corner of the chart to appear.

NOTE ▼

Excel displays a solid line rectangle where you specify the size and shape of the chart on the worksheet. Releasing the mouse button brings up the ChartWizard - Step 1 of 5 dialog box.

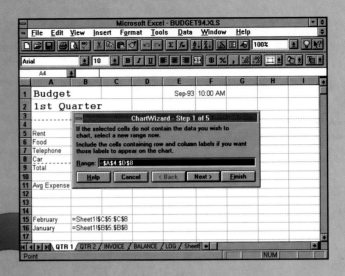

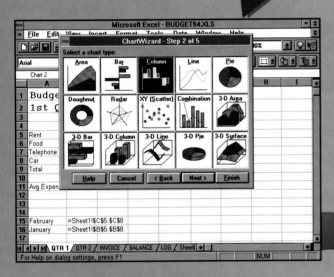

5 Click the **Next** button. This step confirms the selected range—in this case, A4:D8. Excel brings up the ChartWizard - Step 2 of 5 dialog box with chart types. The column chart is the default chart type.

NOTE ▼

The dollar signs indicate an absolute address. See your Microsoft Excel documentation for more information.

6 Click the **Next** button. This step confirms the type of chart—in this case, the column chart. Excel brings up the ChartWizard - Step 3 of 5 dialog box with the formats for the chart type. Column chart 6 is the default format for the column chart type—a column chart with horizontal gridlines. This is the format we want.

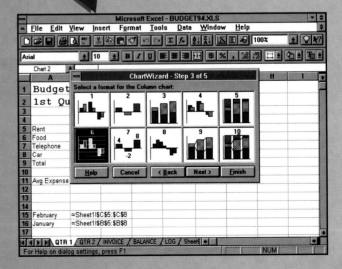

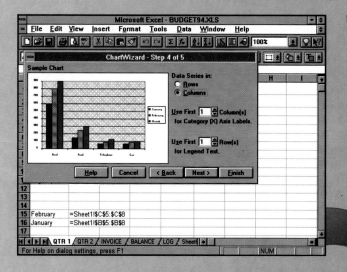

7 Click the **Next** button. This step confirms the format for the chart type—in this case, Column chart 6. Excel displays the Chart-Wizard - Step 4 of 5 dialog box with the sample chart. Notice that the data series is charted in columns. As you can see, each bar represents the values for each month by expense category. We want Excel to use the data series in rows—in this case, each bar will represent the values for each category by month.

8 Click the **Rows** option button. This step changes the plot order to show the data series in rows. Excel redisplays the chart with January, February, and March as the category (X) axis labels. The expense names appear in the legend for the data series.

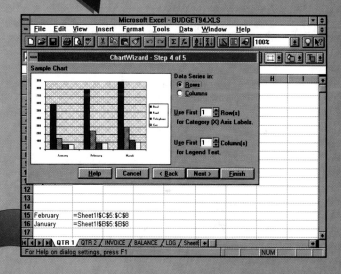

9 Click the **Next** button, which confirms the options for the data series and first column and first row. Excel displays the final dialog box, ChartWizard - Step 5 of 5, with the sample chart again and gives you options for adding a legend and titles. Let's keep the legend that explains the data series and add a chart title.

Task 55: Creating a Chart

10 Click in the **Chart Title** text box or press the Tab key. Then type **1st Quarter Expenses**. This step enters the title for the chart and gives the chart a name. Excel redisplays the chart with the title at the top.

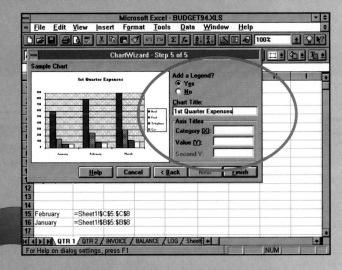

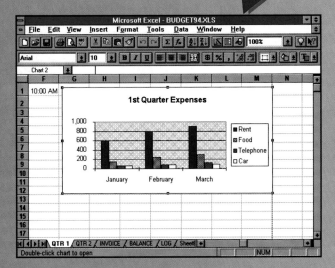

11 Click the **Finish** button. This step creates the new chart on the worksheet. The chart appears in the worksheet at the chosen location. Scroll to the right to see the entire chart. Click the **Save** button on the Standard toolbar to save the file.

WHY WORRY?

You can stop the process of creating an embedded chart with the ChartWizard at any time. Just click the Cancel button in the ChartWizard dialog box. Then start over. If you want to return to the previous ChartWizard dialog box, click the Back button.

Printing a Chart

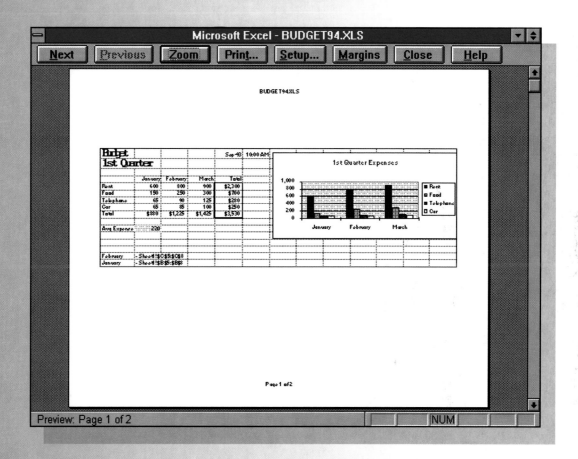

"Why would I do this?"

You can print the embedded chart with its worksheet as you would any worksheet. You might want to print the chart and worksheet together for a presentation. That way, you can easily see trends in a series of values.

Let's print the worksheet and the chart.

Task 56: Printing a Chart

1 Click the **Print Preview** button on the Standard toolbar. Clicking the Print Preview button displays the screen. As you can see, the worksheet and chart appear on-screen in the preview window.

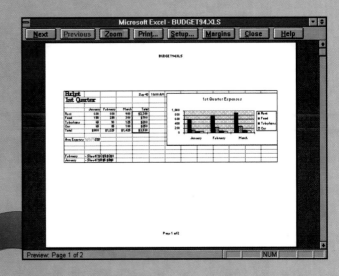

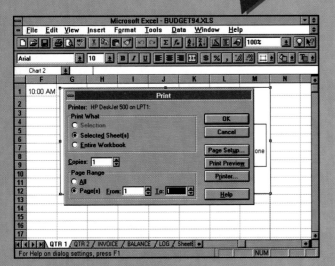

2 Click the **Print** button on the Standard toolbar. Clicking the Print button displays the Print dialog box. From the Page Range options, click the **Page(s)** option button, type **1** in the **From** box, press **Tab**, and type **1** in the **To** box. This step enters the range of pages to print—in this case, only page 1. Click **OK** to confirm your choices. Excel prints the worksheet and the chart.

NOTE ▼

If you are printing a chart on a printer that doesn't print color—for example, a non-color dot matrix printer—you must change the print chart options to print in black and white. Otherwise, you will not get the printout results you want. Select the File Page Setup command; click on the Chart tab to select the Chart options; then select the Print in Black and White option. Then you can print the chart.

WHY WORRY?

During a print job, Excel displays a dialog box on-screen. To stop the print job, click Cancel.

Changing the Chart's Size and Shape

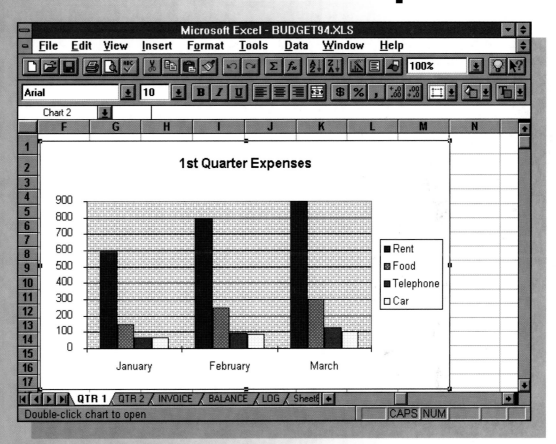

"Why would I do this?"

The size of the embedded chart border that you specify determines the size and shape of the chart in the worksheet. So, if you want to shrink the chart or make it taller, you can move and resize the chart after it's on the worksheet.

Task 57: Changing the Chart's Size and Shape

1 Click cell **F1** and press **Del**. This step deletes the time in cell F1 to make room for widening the chart. Then click anywhere on the chart. This step selects the chart. Excel displays small black squares called *selection handles* on the chart's border. You can use selection handles to resize a chart.

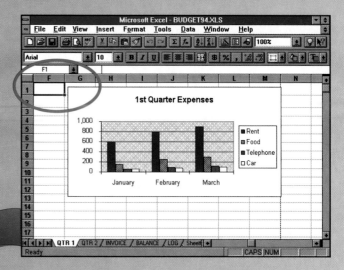

2 Move the mouse pointer to the left middle selection handle and when the cursor becomes a double-headed arrow, drag the chart to the left, aligning the chart with the left edge of column F. This step makes the chart wider.

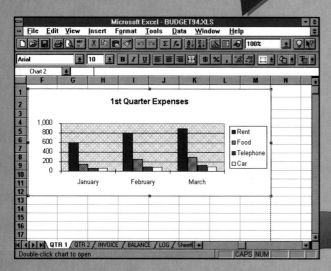

3 Move the mouse pointer to the bottom middle selection handle and when the cursor changes to a double-headed arrow, drag the chart down to the bottom edge of row 17. This step makes the chart taller.

WHY WORRY?

If you don't like the size and shape of the chart, drag the selection handles in the direction you want until you get the desired results.

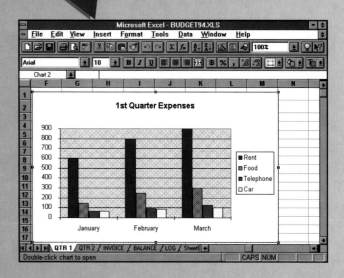

Changing the Chart Type

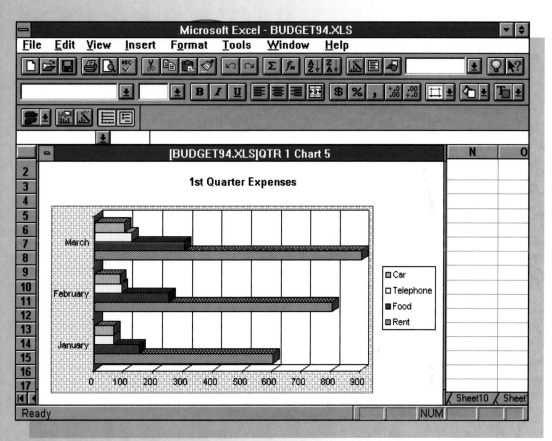

"Why would I do this?"

You can take an existing chart and turn it into a different chart instantly at any time. You will find that certain chart types are best for certain situations. It might be more dramatic, appropriate, or meaningful to display the data in a different type of chart. For example, you can usually spot trends more easily with a line chart, while a pie chart is best for showing parts of a whole. A line chart shows trends over time.

Task 58: Changing the Chart Type

1 Double-click anywhere on the chart. Excel displays the chart in its own window. The Chart toolbar appears above the chart window on the left side of the workbook.

NOTE ▼

If Excel doesn't display the Chart toolbar, choose the View Toolbars command, click the check box next to Chart, then click OK.

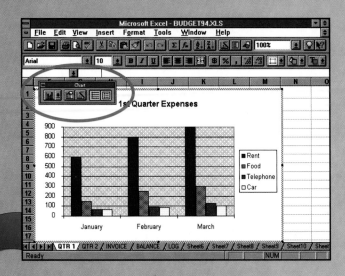

2 Click the down arrow next to the Chart Type button on the Chart toolbar. Choosing the Chart Type button selects the Format Chart Type command. Excel displays a palette of predesigned charts.

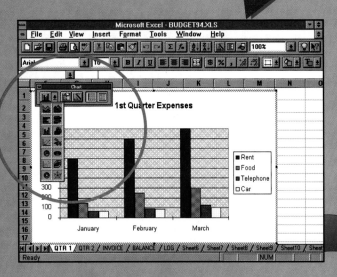

3 In the first column, click the fourth chart from the top. This step selects the chart type—in this case, the line chart. Excel changes the chart to reflect your choice. Notice that the lines represent the expenses by month. It is easier to depict trends in the column chart than in the line chart. So, let's see what the 3-D horizontal column chart looks like.

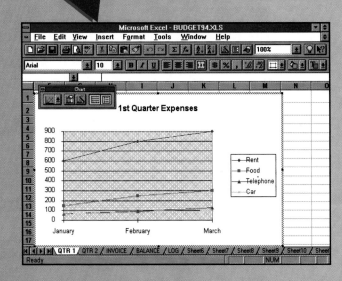

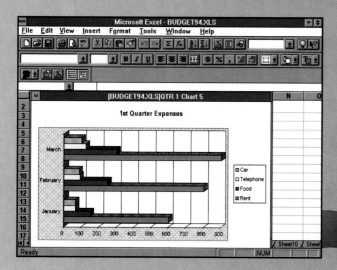

4 Click the down arrow next to the Chart Type button. In the second column, click the second chart from the top. This step selects the 3-D horizontal column chart type. Excel changes the chart to the horizontal column format, showing 3-D horizontal bars. This looks like a good representation for your data; however, let's switch to the area chart.

5 Click the down arrow next to the Chart Type button. In the first column, click the first chart from the top. This step selects the area chart type. Excel changes the chart to the area chart format, showing lines with the areas filled in with color between the lines. Also, the maximum number on the vertical axis scale changed from 900 to 1,600. The area chart doesn't depict the data as well as the column chart. So, let's switch back to the vertical column chart type.

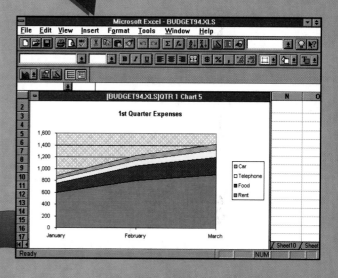

6 Click the down arrow next to the Chart Type button. In the first column, click the third chart from the top. This step selects the column chart type. Excel changes the chart back to the vertical column format.

WHY WORRY?

If the chart type you choose is not what you want, just click another chart type in the Chart Type palette on the Chart toolbar.

Formatting the Title

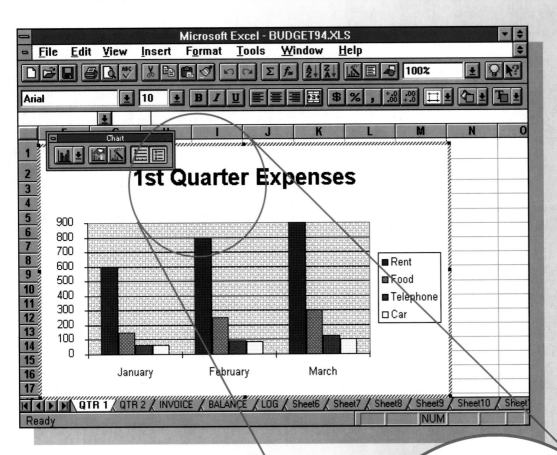

"Why would I do this?"

Excel gives you several formatting options for the text that appears in a chart. You can make the text print vertically, horizontally, or stacked. You can change the font, font size, style, and color of any text. You can also move text anywhere you want on the chart. You might want to change the font for the title to a larger font and boldface the title to draw attention to the title.

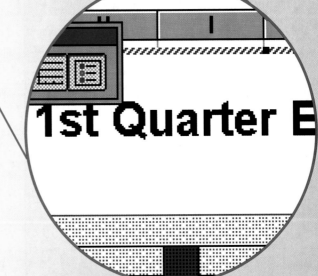

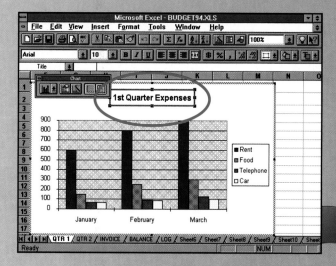

1 Click the title at the top of the chart. A border with selection handles surrounds the title.

2 Click the down arrow next to the Font Size box on the Formatting toolbar. Excel displays a list of font sizes. Click a larger number. Then press **Esc** to deselect the title. In the figure, the new font size is 20.

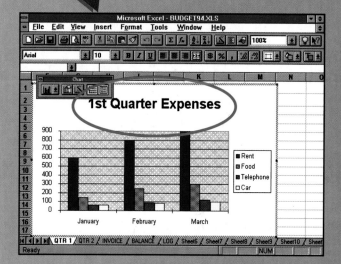

NOTE ▼

The font sizes may vary, depending on the type of printer you have and the fonts installed.

WHY WORRY?

If the new font size is not what you want, repeat the previous steps and choose a different font size. Then press Esc to deselect the title.

TASK 60

Adding a Legend

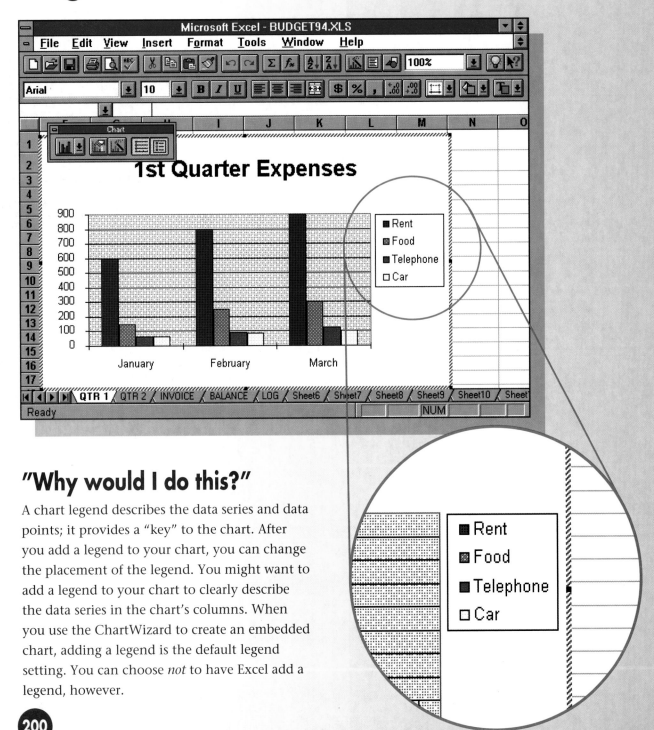

"Why would I do this?"

A chart legend describes the data series and data
points; it provides a "key" to the chart. After
you add a legend to your chart, you can change
the placement of the legend. You might want to
add a legend to your chart to clearly describe
the data series in the chart's columns. When
you use the ChartWizard to create an embedded
chart, adding a legend is the default legend
setting. You can choose *not* to have Excel add a
legend, however.

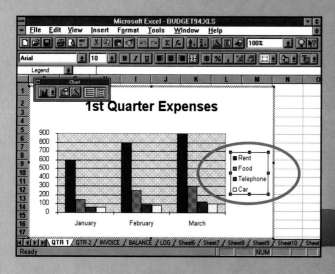

1 Click the legend. This step selects the legend. A border with selection handles (small black squares) surrounds the legend.

2 Move the mouse pointer inside the legend border and drag the legend to the bottom right corner of the chart (as shown in the figure). This step moves the legend to the new location. Now let's try moving it up higher and see how it looks.

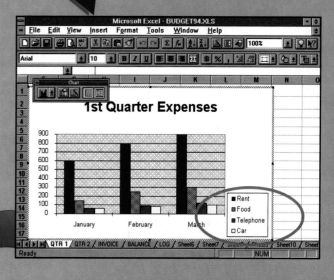

3 Move the mouse pointer inside the legend border and drag the legend to the upper right corner of the plot area, aligning it with the top right edge of the plot area (as shown in the figure). This step moves the legend to the new location.

WHY WORRY?

To remove the legend, click the Legend button on the Chart toolbar.

TASK 61
Adding Gridlines

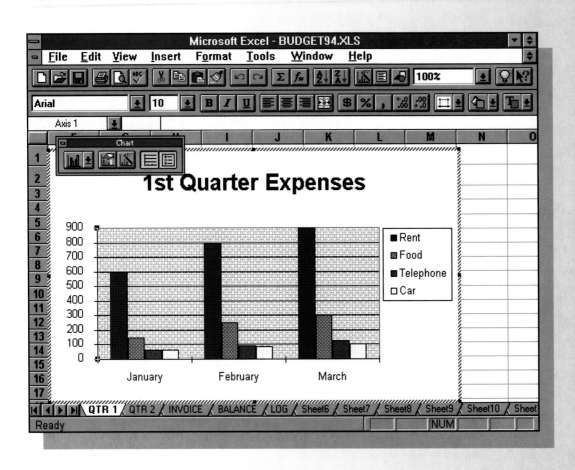

"Why would I do this?"

With Excel, you can also add a grid to your chart. A grid appears in the plot area of the chart. Placing a grid on your chart makes it easier to interpret the chart's data. A grid is useful for emphasizing the vertical scale of the data series.

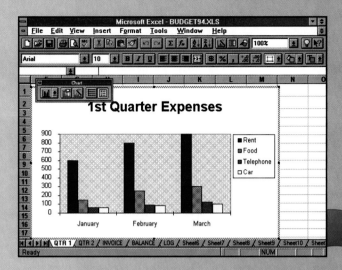

1 Click the **Horizontal Gridlines** button on the Chart toolbar. Clicking the Horizontal Gridlines button selects the Insert Gridlines command and deselects the Major Gridlines option in the Gridlines dialog box. Excel removes the dotted lines across the chart.

2 Click the **Horizontal Gridlines** button on the Chart toolbar again. Clicking the Horizontal Gridlines button selects the Insert Gridlines command and selects the Major Gridlines option in the Gridlines dialog box. Excel displays the dotted lines across the chart.

WHY WORRY?

To remove the gridlines, click the Horizontal Gridlines button again.

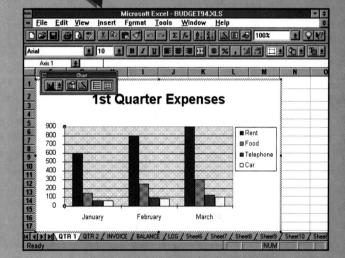

Changing Axis Scales

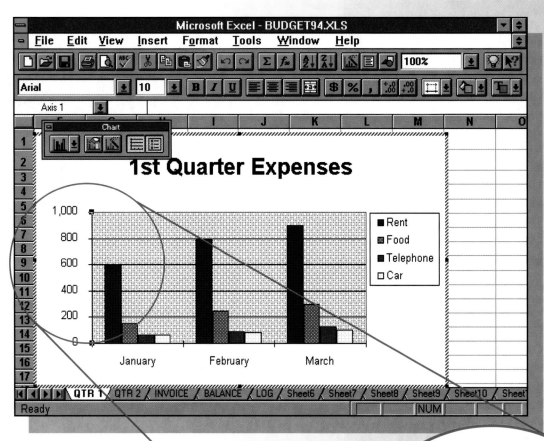

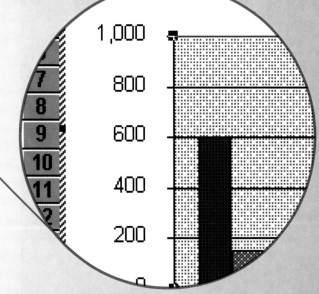

"Why would I do this?"

The vertical axis in an Excel chart is called the *value axis*. Excel automatically scales the value axis for your charts to best fit the minimum and maximum values being charted. But, sometimes you might need to customize the values along the vertical or horizontal axis. Perhaps you want to display fewer numbers in larger increments on the value axis.

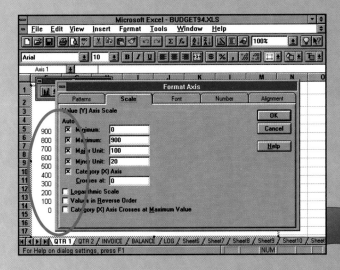

1 Click the vertical axis line. This step selects the value axis. Selection boxes (small black squares) appear at each end of the value axis.

2 Double-click the vertical axis line. Excel displays the Format Axis dialog box. Click the **Scale** tab to display the Scale options.

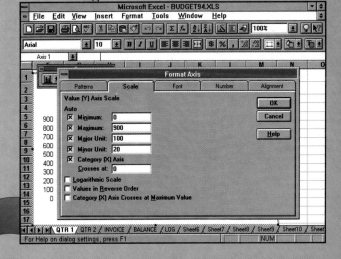

NOTE ▼

The Format Axis dialog box contains various options for changing the axes. For more information on these options, refer to your Microsoft Excel documentation.

3 Double-click in the **Maximum** text box and type **1000**. This step enters the high value on the value axis—in this case, 1000. Notice that the Auto check box is cleared.

Task 62: Changing Axis Scales

4 Double-click in the **Major Unit** text box and type **200**. This step enters the interval between values on the value axis—in this case, 200. Notice that the Auto check box is cleared.

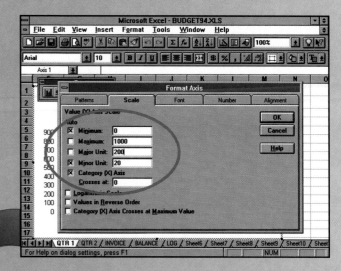

5 Click **OK**. This step confirms your choices. As you can see that the highest value at the top of the vertical axis is 1000 and the interval between values is 200.

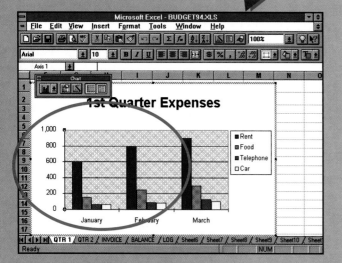

WHY WORRY?

If you don't get the scale numbers you want, just click the Undo button on the Standard toolbar. If you want to clear the settings and return to the original default values, select the appropriate Auto check boxes.

Formatting the Axes

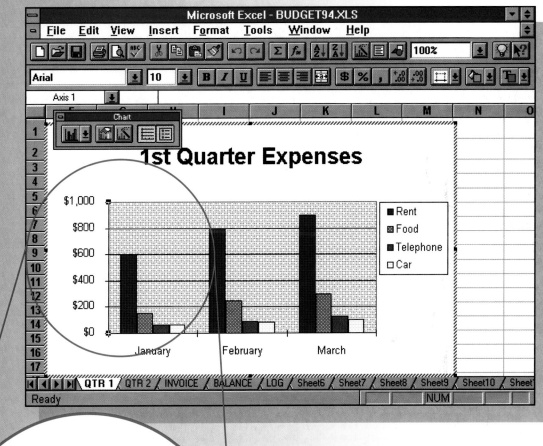

"Why would I do this?"

You can change the look of the scale indicators on the axes. For example, you can change the style, color, and weight of the axis line. You can change the format of the numbers that appear on the axis scale by adding dollars signs, decimal points, commas, and percent signs.

Let's add dollar signs to the values on the vertical axis in our column chart. Then let's change the font for the values on the vertical axis.

207

Task 63: Formatting the Axes

1 Click the vertical axis line, if necessary. This step selects the value axis. Selection boxes (small black squares) appear at each end of the value axis.

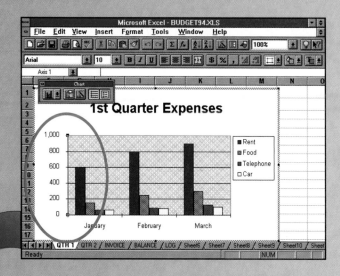

2 Double-click the vertical axis line. Excel displays the Format Axis dialog box. Click the **Number** tab to display the Number options.

NOTE ▼

You can change the Patterns, Scale, Font, Number, and Alignment options in the dialog box. See your Microsoft Excel documentation for complete information.

3 Scroll down to the bottom of the Category list. When you see Currency, click it. This step selects the Currency category. Notice that the first format in the Format Codes list is currently selected. This number format adds dollar signs and commas with zero decimal places. The sample $1,000 appears at the bottom of the dialog box. This is the number format we want.

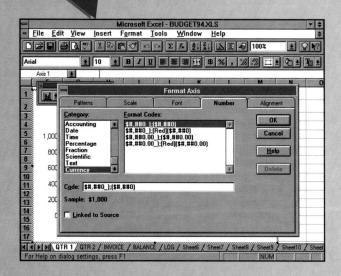

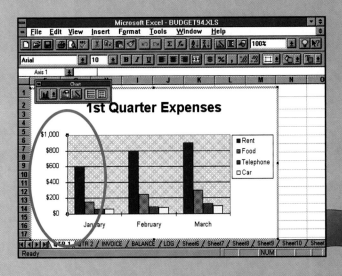

4 Click **OK**. This step confirms your choice. Excel adds dollar signs to the values on the vertical axis scale.

5 Double-click the vertical axis line. Excel displays the Format Axis dialog box. Click the **Font** tab to display the Font options. Then click any font in the list. In the figure, the new font is Courier.

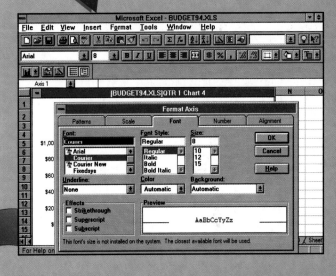

6 Click **OK**. This step confirms your choice. Excel changes the font for the values on the vertical axis scale.

WHY WORRY?

If you don't get the results you want, click the Undo button on the Standard toolbar. Then repeat the previous steps and choose a different number format.

209

TASK 64

Changing the Patterns of Data Series

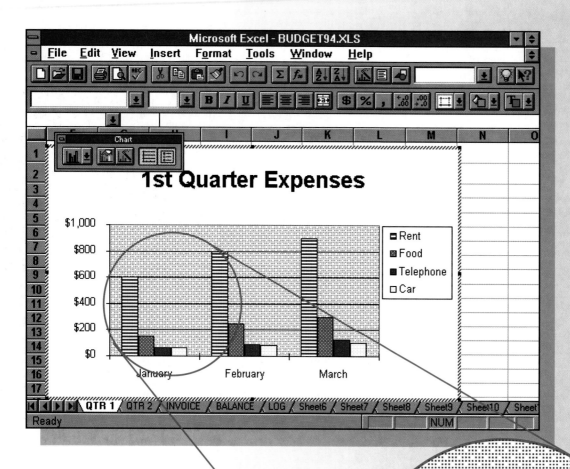

"Why would I do this?"

You might want to change the colors and patterns of the data series for special effects. When you change the patterns of data series, you might find some patterns and colors more attractive than others. For example, you might want to remove all patterns and use only color.

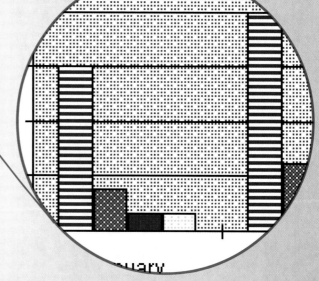

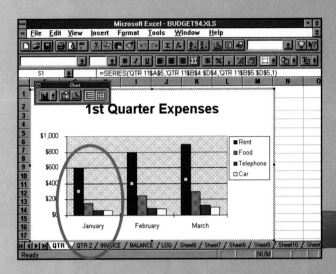

1 Click the first data series, (the bar that represents the rent for January). This step selects all the bars that represent the rent for each month. Small squares appear in each of the bars. These squares are called *selection boxes*.

2 Double-click any data series. Double-clicking a data series displays the Patterns tab in the Format Data Series dialog box.

NOTE ▼

The Border options on the Patterns tab affect the perimeter of the selected element, including the style, color, and weight of the border line. The Area options control the inside of the element, such as its pattern and color.

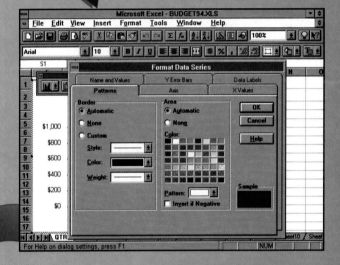

3 From the **Area** options, click the down arrow next to the **Pattern** text box. Excel displays a palette of patterns and colors.

4 In the first column of the palette, click the second pattern from the top. This step selects the horizontal striped pattern. The sample appears in the lower right corner of the dialog box.

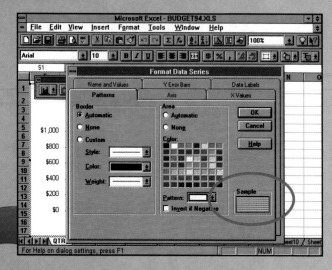

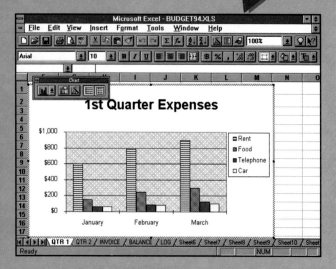

5 Click **OK**. Then press **Esc** to deselect the data series. This step confirms your choice. Excel displays the bars in the horizontal striped pattern with the default color—in this case, royal blue. Notice that the legend contains the new pattern for Rent.

WHY WORRY?

To remove the pattern from a data series, click the Undo button on the Standard toolbar. Then repeat the previous steps and choose a different pattern or a color.

Changing the Category Labels

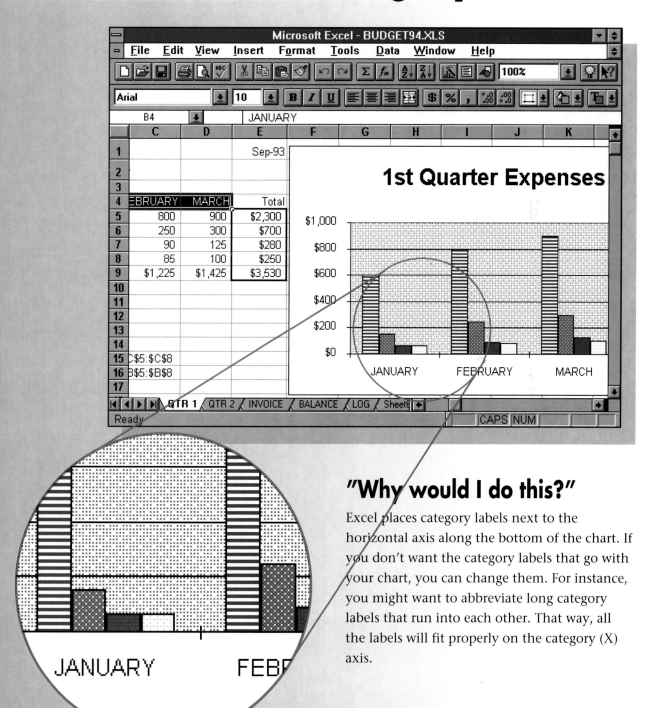

"Why would I do this?"

Excel places category labels next to the horizontal axis along the bottom of the chart. If you don't want the category labels that go with your chart, you can change them. For instance, you might want to abbreviate long category labels that run into each other. That way, all the labels will fit properly on the category (X) axis.

Task 65: Changing the Category Labels

1 Click any cell to deselect the chart. Then press **Ctrl+Home** to return to cell A1. Now you can see the worksheet. Select cells **B4** to **D4**. This step selects the range B4:D4 where we will enter the category labels we want in the chart.

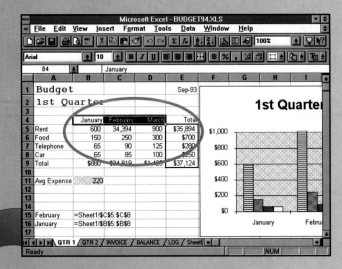

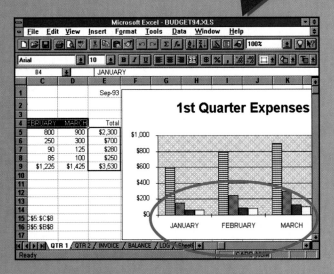

2 Type the data that appears in the figure so that your computer screen matches the one in the book. Then scroll to the right so that you can see the chart. As you type the data, Excel instantly updates the category labels in the chart to reflect the changes in the worksheet. The new category labels appear at the bottom of the chart.

NOTE ▼

The data in the cells may overlap when they are filled with capital letters.

WHY WORRY?

If you entered the wrong category labels, just delete the old category labels in the worksheet, and then enter new ones.

214

Adding Text Labels

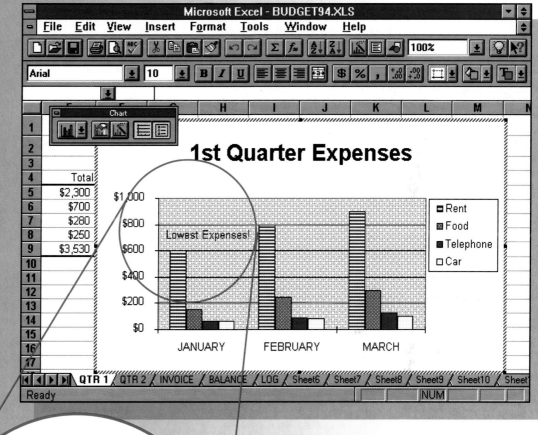

"Why would I do this?"

Adding text labels makes the chart's data more meaningful and may accentuate a certain bar, line, or slice of pie in the chart. You might want to add a text label to point out the highest or lowest value in the chart.

In our chart, let's create a text label, "Lowest Expenses!", and place it next to the January data series.

Task 66: Adding Text Labels

1 Scroll right to see the entire chart. Then double-click anywhere in the chart to select it.

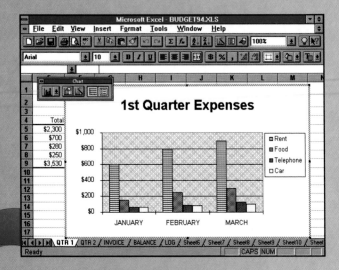

2 Click the **Text Box** button on the Standard toolbar. Clicking the Text Box button displays a cross-hair pointer. On the chart, below the title, drag the cross-hair pointer to draw a rectangular box, as shown in the figure. Excel adds a text box to the chart that is surrounded by white selection handles; the selection boxes indicate that the box is not moveable. The insertion point appears in the white box. This box will contain temporary text as a place holder.

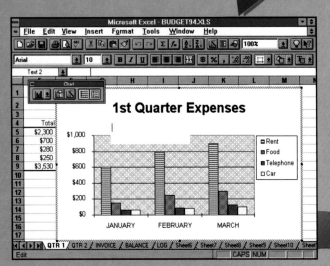

3 Type **Lowest Expenses!**. This step enters the text for the label. Lowest Expenses! appears on the chart.

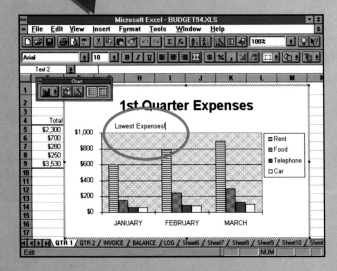

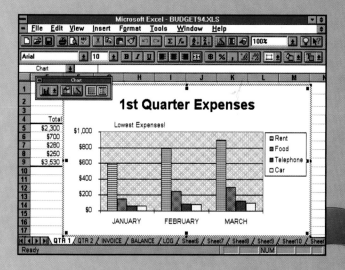

4 Click outside the text box. This step confirms that you are finished typing text.

5 Click Lowest Expenses! A border with selection handles surrounds the text. If necessary, use the selection handles to shrink the box so that it is the same size as the text. Then move the mouse pointer to the box's border and drag the text box above the first set of bars. Finally, press **Esc** to deselect the text box. This step repositions the text label where you want it to appear on the chart—in this case, above the data series for January.

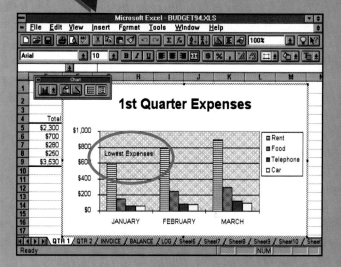

NOTE ▼

To make the label easier to see, you can add bold to the label. Just click the label, then click the Bold button on the Formatting toolbar.

WHY WORRY?

To remove a text label from the chart, click the text label to select it, and then press Del.

Using Chart AutoFormat

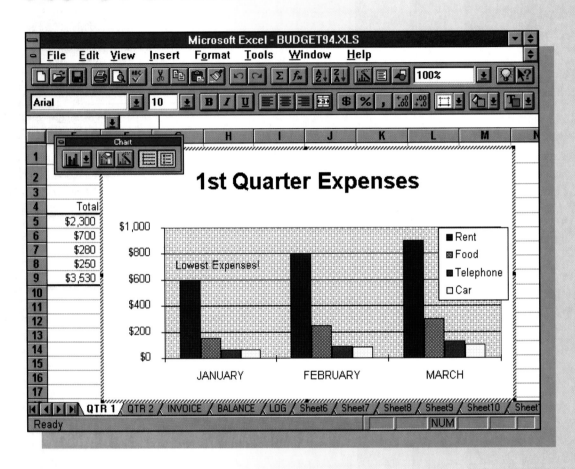

"Why would I do this?"

In Excel 5, you can now apply a set of predefined formats to a selected chart on the worksheet. Previously, you applied one format at a time to a selected element. But now you can apply a collection of formats supplied by Excel all at once. The chart formats help you create professional-looking charts.

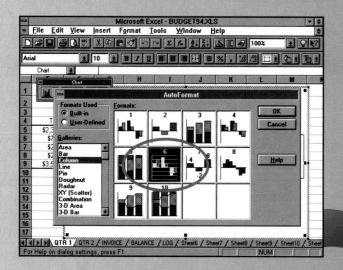

1 Choose the **Format AutoFormat** command. Excel displays the AutoFormat dialog box. A list of chart types and a palette of chart formats appear in the box. The Column chart 6 format is currently selected. This is the format we want.

2 Click **OK**. This step confirms your choice. Excel changes the chart to the new format. Note the Rent bars changed back to a solid color and the legend appears in the upper right corner on the plot area. Click the **Save** button on the Standard toolbar to save the file.

WHY WORRY?

To remove the format, click the Undo button on the Standard toolbar. Then repeat the previous steps and choose a different chart type and/or format.

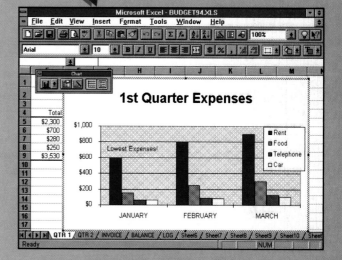

PART VIII

Sample Documents

▼ Create a Company Sales Report

▼ Create a Departmental Budget

▼ Create a Memo with a Table

▼ Create a Column Chart

▼ Create an Expense Report
and a Column Chart

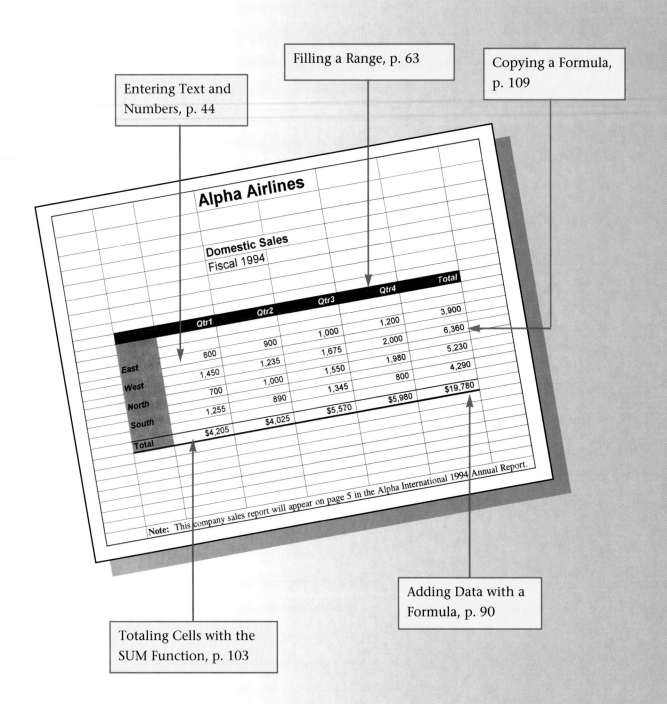

Filling a Range, p. 63

Copying a Formula, p. 109

Entering Text and Numbers, p. 44

Alpha Airlines

Domestic Sales
Fiscal 1994

	Qtr1	Qtr2	Qtr3	Qtr4	Total
East	800	900	1,000	1,200	3,900
West	1,450	1,235	1,675	2,000	6,360
North	700	1,000	1,550	1,980	5,230
South	1,255	890	1,345	800	4,290
Total	$4,205	$4,025	$5,570	$5,980	$19,780

Note: This company sales report will appear on page 5 in the Alpha International 1994 Annual Report.

Adding Data with a Formula, p. 90

Totaling Cells with the SUM Function, p. 103

Create a Company Sales Report

1 Type the title, column headings, row headings, and numbers. See this task for help on this step:

2 Enter a formula to add the first column of numbers. These tasks cover addition formulas:

3 Copy the formula across the total row. These tasks cover copying a formula:

4 Change the format of the entire worksheet to the Classic 2 Format. See this task:

5 Save and print the sales report. See these tasks on saving and printing:

Displaying Dollar Signs, Commas, and Percent Signs, p. 140

Entering Text and Numbers, p. 44

Adding Borders, p. 160

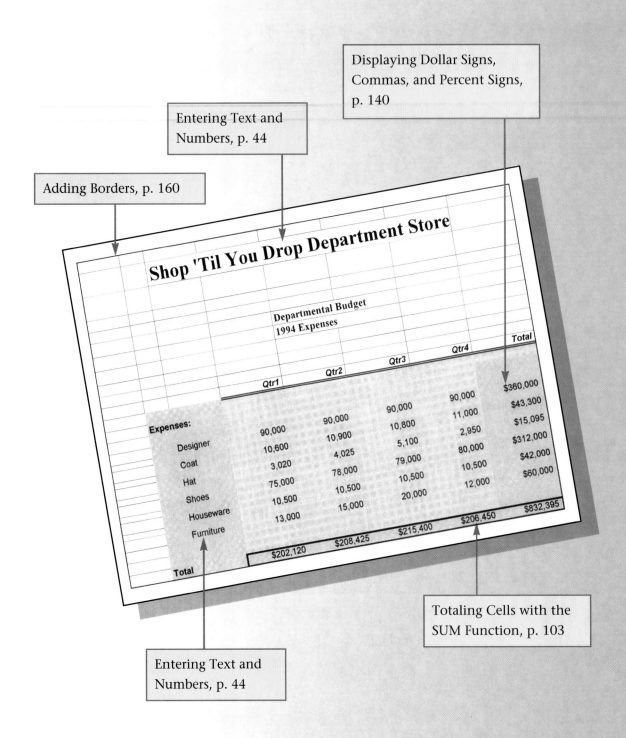

Shop 'Til You Drop Department Store

Departmental Budget
1994 Expenses

	Qtr1	Qtr2	Qtr3	Qtr4	Total
Expenses:					$360,000
Designer	90,000	90,000	90,000	90,000	$43,300
Coat	10,600	10,900	10,800	11,000	$15,095
Hat	3,020	4,025	5,100	2,950	$312,000
Shoes	75,000	78,000	79,000	80,000	$42,000
Houseware	10,500	10,500	10,500	10,500	$60,000
Furniture	13,000	15,000	20,000	12,000	
Total	$202,120	$208,425	$215,400	$206,450	$832,395

Totaling Cells with the SUM Function, p. 103

Entering Text and Numbers, p. 44

Create a Departmental Budget

1 Type the information in the budget worksheet. See these tasks for help on this step:

Entering Text and Numbers   *Task 9, p. 44*

Totaling Cells with the SUM Function   *Task 29, p. 103*

Filling a Range   *Task 16, p. 63*

2 Format the numbers for each quarter with commas to zero decimal places. Format the numbers in the total row with dollar signs and zero decimal places. See this task:

*Displaying Dollar Signs, Commas,
and Percent Signs*   *Task 40, p. 140*

3 Insert a double underline border beneath the column headings. Also, add an outline border to the numbers in the total row. See this task:

Adding Borders   *Task 47, p. 160*

4 Change the font color of the column and row headings to bright blue. See this task:

Formatting Cell Contents   *Task 45, p. 154*

5 Add light gray shading to the numbers in each column except for the last row (total row). Then change the color of the cells in the total row and the total column to aqua. See this task:

Shading Cells   *Task 46, p. 158*

6 Save and print the budget. See these tasks on saving and printing:

Saving a Workbook   *Task 33, p. 120*

Printing the Worksheet   *Task 54, p. 179*

Part VIII: Sample Documents

Formatting Cell
Contents, p. 154

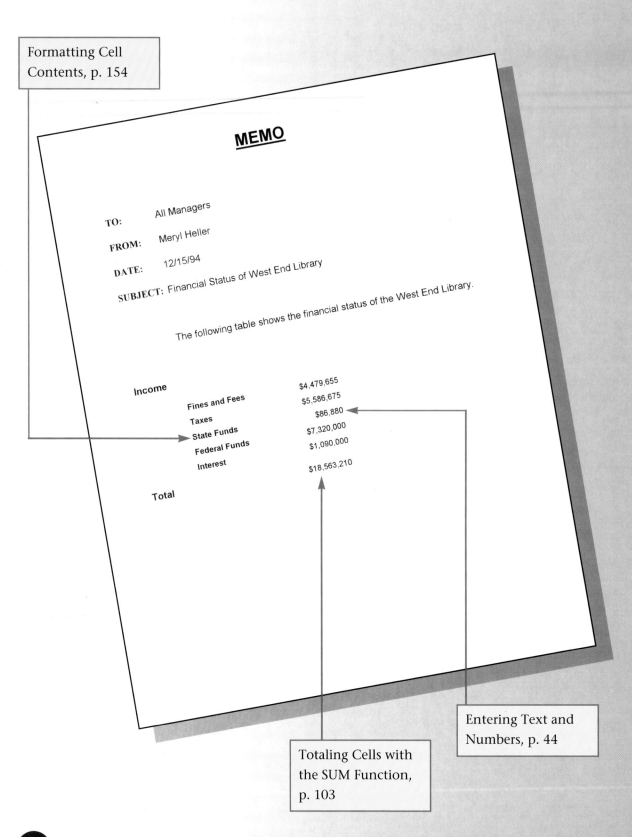

MEMO

TO: All Managers

FROM: Meryl Heller

DATE: 12/15/94

SUBJECT: Financial Status of West End Library

The following table shows the financial status of the West End Library.

Income	
Fines and Fees	$4,479,655
Taxes	$5,586,675
State Funds	$86,880
Federal Funds	$7,320,000
Interest	$1,090,000
	$18,563,210
Total	

Entering Text and
Numbers, p. 44

Totaling Cells with
the SUM Function,
p. 103

Create a Memo with a Table

1 Type the memo including the table. See this task for help on this step:

Entering Text and Numbers   *Task 9, p. 44*

2 Create a SUM formula to add the numbers. See this task:

Totaling Cells with the SUM Function   *Task 29, p. 103*

3 Boldface and underline the title, MEMO. Then change the font for the memo headings to Times New Roman 12 point. Then boldface the memo headings. Also, boldface the headings and subheadings in the table. This task covers font changes, bold, and underline:

Formatting Cell Contents   *Task 45, p. 154*

4 Save and print the memo. See these tasks on saving and printing:

Saving a Workbook   *Task 33, p. 120*

Printing the Worksheet   *Task 54, p. 179*

Formatting the Title,
p. 198

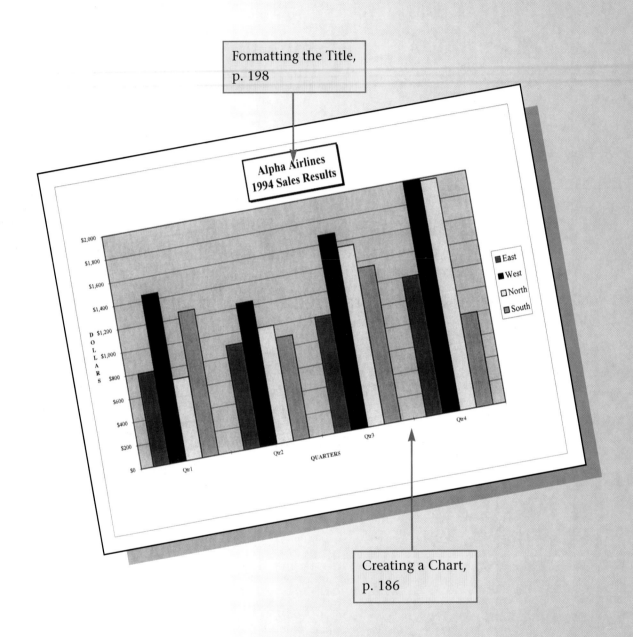

Alpha Airlines
1994 Sales Results

Creating a Chart,
p. 186

Create a Column Chart

1 Using the company sales report, create a column chart on a separate sheet to show quarterly sales by territory. The data you want to chart includes the column headings, row headings, and the sales figures. Do not include the totals. See these tasks for help on this step:

Selecting Cells	*Task 8, p. 35*
Moving Between Worksheets	*Task 6, p. 29*
Creating a Chart	*Task 55, p. 186*

2 Change the font for the chart title to Times New Roman 18. Also, boldface the title. See this task for help on this step:

Formatting the Title	*Task 59, p. 198*

3 Save and print the chart. See these tasks on saving and printing:

Saving a Workbook	*Task 33, p. 120*
Printing a Chart	*Task 56, p. 191*

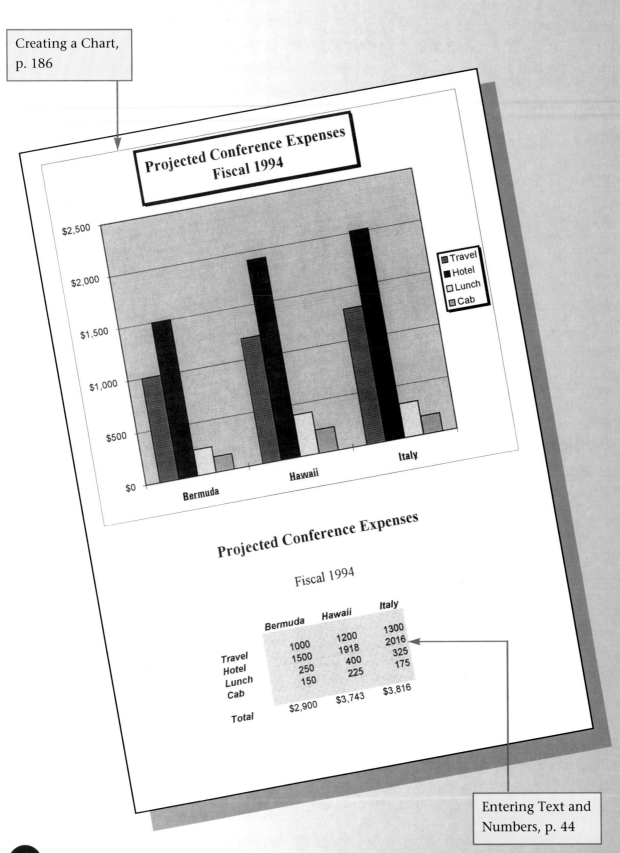

Creating a Chart, p. 186

Projected Conference Expenses
Fiscal 1994

Projected Conference Expenses

Fiscal 1994

	Bermuda	Hawaii	Italy
Travel	1000	1200	1300
Hotel	1500	1918	2016
Lunch	250	400	325
Cab	150	225	175
Total	$2,900	$3,743	$3,816

Entering Text and Numbers, p. 44

Create an Expense Report and a Column Chart

1 Type the expense report in the worksheet. See this task for help on this step:

Entering Text and Numbers	*Task 9, p. 44*

2 Enter a formula to subtract expenses from the income. See this task:

Subtracting Data with a Formula	*Task 26, p. 94*

3 Copy the formula across the total row. These tasks cover copying a formula:

Filling a Range	*Task 16, p. 63*
Copying a Formula	*Task 31, p. 109*

4 Select the data you want to chart: the column headings, row headings, and the expenses. Do not include the totals. Be sure to plot the data series in rows. See these tasks for help on this step:

Selecting Cells	*Task 8, p. 35*
Creating a Chart	*Task 55, p. 186*

5 Create a column chart on the worksheet. See this task:

Creating a Chart	*Task 55, p. 186*

6 Save and print the balance sheet and the column chart. See these tasks on saving and printing:

Saving a Workbook	*Task 33, p. 120*
Printing a Chart	*Task 56, p. 191*

PART IX

Reference

▼ Quick Reference

▼ Toolbar Guide

Quick Reference

If you cannot remember how to access a particular feature, use this quick list to find the appropriate command. For more detailed information, see the tasks in Parts I through VII of this book.

Feature	Command	Shortcut Key
Alignment	Format Cells (Alignment tab)	Ctrl+1 (Alignment tab)
Border	Format Cells (Border tab)	Ctrl+1 (Border tab)
Close File	File Close	(none)
Column Delete	Edit Delete Entire Column	(none)
Column Hide	Format Column Hide	(none)
Column Insert	Insert Columns	(none)
Column Width	Format Column Width	(none)
Copy	Edit Copy	Ctrl+C
Edit Cell	(none)	F2
Exit	File Exit	Alt+F4
Font	Format Cells (Font tab)	Ctrl+1 (Font tab)
Format Numbers	Format Cells (Number tab)	Ctrl+1 (Number tab)
Go To	Edit Go To	F5
Help	Help	F1
Move	Edit Cut, then Edit Paste	Ctrl+X, then Ctrl+V
New File	File New	Ctrl+N
Open File	File Open	Ctrl+O
Page Break	Insert Page Break	(none)
Preview	File Print Preview	(none)
Print	File Print	Ctrl+P
Range Fill	Edit Fill Series	(none)
Range Name	Insert Name Define	(none)

Feature	Command	Shortcut Key
Replace	Edit Replace	Ctrl+H
Row Delete	Edit Delete Entire Row	(none)
Row Height	Format Row Height	(none)
Row Hide	Format Row Hide	(none)
Row Insert	Insert Rows	(none)
Save	File Save	Ctrl+S
Save As	File Save As	(none)
Shade	Format Cells (Patterns tab)	Ctrl+1 (Patterns tab)
Sort Data	Data Sort	(none)
Undo	Edit Undo	Ctrl+Z

Toolbar Guide

The Standard and Formatting toolbars appear at the top of the Excel screen and contain many tools that let you accomplish Excel tasks more quickly. To use a toolbar button, simply click the button.

Standard Toolbar

Button	Name	Purpose
	New Workbook	Creates a new workbook
	Open	Opens a workbook
	Save	Saves a workbook
	Print	Prints a worksheet
	Print Preview	Previews a print job
	Spelling	Checks the spelling in a worksheet
	Cut	Cuts a range to the Clipboard
	Copy	Copies a range to the Clipboard

(continues)

Standard Toolbar (continued)

Button	Name	Purpose
	Paste	Pastes a range
	Format Painter	Copies formats
	Undo	Undoes the preceding action
	Repeat	Repeats the preceding action
	AutoSum	Inserts a SUM formula
	Function Wizard	Inserts and edits functions
	Sort Ascending	Sorts data in ascending order
	Sort Descending	Sorts data in descending order
	ChartWizard	Accesses the ChartWizard
	Text Box	Inserts a text box
	Drawing	Displays the Drawing toolbar
100%	Zoom Control	Controls the display of a worksheet
	TipWizard	Provides tips on Excel operations
	Help	Provides on-screen Help about Excel

Formatting Toolbar

Button	Name	Purpose
Arial	Font	Changes font
10	Font Size	Changes font size
B	Bold	Makes cell contents bold
I	Italic	Makes cell contents italic
U	Underline	Makes cell contents underlined
	Align Left	Aligns cell entries to the left
	Center	Centers entries in a cell
	Align Right	Aligns cell entries to the right
	Center Across Columns	Centers text across columns

Button	Name	Purpose
$	Currency Style	Adds dollar signs to numbers
%	Percent Style	Adds percent signs to numbers
,	Comma Style	Adds commas to numbers
Increase Decimal icon	Increase Decimal	Adds one decimal place to number
Decrease Decimal icon	Decrease Decimal	Removes one decimal place from number
Borders icon	Borders	Adds a border to a selected range
Color icon	Color	Adds a color to a range
Font Color icon	Font Color	Adds color to a font

Index

Index

Index

D

data
  aligning, 138-139
  editing, 50-52
  entering in worksheets, 41-45
  erasing from cells, 53-54
  filling ranges, 61-62
  finding and replacing, 79-81
  moving between cells, 58-60
  overwriting, 48-49
  sorting, 77-78
data series, charts, 184, 210-212
dates
  aligning, 138-139
  entering in worksheets, 45
  formats, 40-41
    changing, 146-149
decimal places, specifying, 143-145
Decrease Decimal button, Formatting toolbar, 144
Del key (erase cell contents), 53-54
deleting
  columns, 63-65
  page breaks, 168-169
  range names, 115
  rows, 63-65
dialog boxes
  ChartWizard, 188-189
  Format Axis, 205, 208-209
  Format Cells, 148-149
  Format Data Series, 211
  Go To, 33
  Help button, 23
  How To, 23
  Number Format, 136, 149
  Open, 127-129
  Options, 163
  Page Setup, 166-167, 171, 173-174
  Paste Name, 115
  Print, 181
  Rename Sheet, 132
  Replace, 80-81
  Save As, 121
  Search, 129-130
  Spelling, 84-85
  Summary Info, 121
division (/) operator, 102
division formulas, 100-102
documents, *see* worksheets
dollar sign ($), formatting with, 140-142
double-clicking, 15

E

editing cell contents, 50-52
equals sign (=), formulas, 91
erasing cell contents, 53-54
Esc key (canceling selections), 18
exiting Excel, 14-15

F

filling ranges, 61-62
finding, 119
  and replacing data, 79-81
  workbooks, 128-130
First Tab scrolling button, 31
Font box, Formatting toolbar, 155
Font Size box, Formatting toolbar, 156
fonts, 137
footers, 174-176
Format Painter button, Standard toolbar, 150-151
formatting
  aligning data, 138-139
  axes, 207-209
  borders around cells, 160-161
  cell contents, 154-157
  charts, 218-219

Index

M

N

O

P

R

range coordinates, 12
ranges, 12
  deleting names, 115
  filling, 61-62
  going to specific, 32-34
  naming, 112-115
  selecting, 35-36
  see also cells
references, cell, 89
relative addressing, 111
renaming sheets, 119, 131-133
replacing data, 79-81
rows
  headings, 40
    freezing, 69-71
    printing, 172-173
  hiding/displaying, 72-73
  inserting/deleting, 63-65

S

sample worksheets, 222-231
Save button, Standard toolbar, 121
saving
  charts, 190
  workbooks, 118, 120-121
scaling axes, 204-206
scroll arrows, 27
scroll bars, 26-28
scroll boxes, 28
scrolling window panes, 76
selecting
  cells/ranges, 35-36
  commands from shortcut menus, 16-18
  print areas, 170-171
  toolbar buttons, 19-20
shading cells, 158-159

sheets, 12
  chart sheets, 184
  renaming, 119, 131-133
shortcut menus, 13
  Clear Contents, 18
  commands, 16-18
sizing charts, 193-194
Sort Ascending button, Standard toolbar, 78
sorting data, 77-78
spell checking, 82-85
Spelling button, Standard toolbar, 84
splitting worksheets, 74-76
Standard toolbar, 5-6
starting Excel, 14-15
subtraction formulas, 94-96
SUM function, 88, 103-105
summing data, 90-93, 103-105
switching between worksheets, 29-31

T

tab scrolling buttons, 29-31
tab split box, 28
text
  aligning, 138-139
  entering, 41-45
  formatting in charts, 198-199
  sorting, 77-78
  spell checking, 82-85
  see also data
Text Box button (Standard toolbar), 216
text labels, 215-217
tick marks, 185
tiling windows, 119
times
  aligning, 138-139
  entering in worksheets, 45
  formats, 41, 146-149
Tip Help button, TipWizard toolbar, 25
TipWizard button, Standard toolbar, 24

Index

TipWizard toolbar, 24-25
titles, formatting in charts, 198-199
toolbars, 13
    selecting buttons, 19-20
    TipWizard, 24
turning off gridlines, 162-163

U

Undo button, Standard toolbar, 47
undoing, 46-47
    cell/range selection, 36
    erased data, 54
    going to wrong cells/ranges, 34
    last entry, 24
    typing errors, 44
unfreezing column/row headings, 71

V

value axis, 184, 204-205
values, 40-41
    aligning, 138-139
    calculating averages, 106-108
    decimal places, specifying, 143-145
    dividing, 100-102
    entering in worksheets, 41-45
    formatting, 140-142
    multiplying, 97-99
    subtracting, 94-96
    summing, 90-93, 103-105
    see also data
views, changing, 66-68

W

windows
    Help, 22
    tiling, 119
workbooks, 12
    closing, 122-123
    creating, 122, 124-125
    finding, 128-130
    naming, 121
    opening, 122, 126-127
        multiple, 118-119
    saving, 118, 120-121
worksheets, 12
    entering data, 41-45
    formatting, 136-137
    navigating, 12-13, 26-28
    printing, 166-167, 179-181
    samples, 222-231
    splitting, 74-76
    switching between, 29-31
    zooming, 66-68

X-Y-Z

X axis, 185
X, formula bar, 43

Y axis, 184

Zoom Control box, Standard toolbar, 67-68
zooming worksheets, 66-68